100

THINGS TO DO IN

ILLINOIS

BEFORE YOU

DIE

Allerton Retreat Center Formal Gardens, Monticello

100 THINGS TO DO IN ILLINOIS BEFORE YOU DIE

MELANIE HOLMES

REEDY PRESS

Reedy Press
PO Box 5131
St. Louis, MO 63139, USA
www.reedypress.com

Library of Congress Control Number: 2022950147
ISBN: 9781681064420

Design by Jill Halpin
Photos by author unless otherwise noted.

Printed in the United States of America
23 24 25 26 27 5 4 3 2

DEDICATION

To my first travel companions, my mom and siblings.
To my husband, Rob, with whom I've traveled
30 years (and counting).
To my kids, who have ridden 20 hours in hot cars
and spelunked and slept in muggy tents
and scared away bobcats with noise.
Love to all those who've been
my travel companions (where next?).

Great River Road, north of Alton

CONTENTS

Music and Entertainment

Sports and Recreation

Culture and History

Fabyan Japanese Garden, Geneva

ACKNOWLEDGMENTS

Always, I thank my family first. Beginning with my mother, Nedine Lemenager Bowman, who took me on my first big trip when I was seven, and for uttering the words—over and over—"Go while you feel like it, because someday you won't feel like it." Hear! Hear! Mom! And thank you.

My husband, Rob, is perhaps the best travel companion a person can have. As ex-Navy (Navy Chief Navy Pride!), he is happiest when there's water nearby (lakes, rivers, oceans), but in the big picture, he is happy so long as we are together. He loves hiking, relaxing, exploring, and he even likes just sitting in a big city library reading about Al Capone (we did the latter on our fourth anniversary). If not for him, my career as an author would never have happened. The words "thank you" are not enough, but thank you, Rob—je t'aime!

When my children were the ages when I controlled their schedules, I schlepped them all over the country—from New York and Virginia to Tennessee and Mississippi. We've camped and hiked and biked and got sunburned and had the biggest bugs ever divebomb our heads at dusk in Kentucky! They're adults now, and they still join in creating memories with me when they can. To them, I offer deep gratitude for saying "yes" whenever possible. Time is a commodity, and I appreciate every moment more than I can say.

To other travel partners (you know who you are), thank you for joining in the fun. From day trips to cruise ships to mountain passes and cabins tucked into campgrounds, it has been a blast. In those ways, you contributed to this book, too. To Nitya, who specifically asked me to list some of my Illinois jaunts, here you go! To Jo-Elle, your honesty over the years helped me to write with greater intention; thank you.

To Josh Stevens, owner of Reedy Press, thank you for that first positive email. To Amanda Doyle, who set me on this particular path, and whose example I followed for writing a Reedy statewide book. To Barb, Chelcie, Morgan, and all those at Reedy who guided me through the process of bringing out this book, thank you for your professionalism, expertise, kindness, and good humor.

White bison,
Wildlife Prairie Park, Hanna City

Emanate by Josh Garber; Goldman-Kuenz
Sculpture Park at Cedarhurst Center for the Arts, Mount Vernon

PREFACE

The need for this book became apparent during the initial shutdowns of the 2020 COVID-19 pandemic. With theaters and shopping malls shuttered, many people suffered from cabin fever, even during beautiful weather. But staying inside is not how some people are built. Rather than sit home weekend after weekend, my husband and I took to the road. Sometimes we went just a mile or two and discovered a hidden waterfall. Other times, we drove farther. As we did, we wanted to obey Illinois's mandates by staying within the state's borders, so we traveled from our home in the suburbs of Chicago to the southern tip of Illinois. There, we roamed among historic Fort Massac, we visited the "hometown" of Superman, and we investigated a cave along the Ohio River that once housed river pirates. On that trip, we slept in an A-Frame just steps from the Ohio River. The entire trip was a dream for two—me and my husband, who is my favorite travel partner in the whole world.

Other drives didn't take us far. For example, just a half-hour from our home is an Indian mound (gravesite). We visited it on a clear winter day, snow covering the mound like a blanket, with a backdrop of the Des Plaines River and an old abandoned barn. Speaking of barns, another of our drives took us to Macomb in central Illinois, where we followed their barn trail. I already knew I liked barns, but that trail achieved a whole new level of love for these historic (and vanishing) architectural beauties.

My mother planted the notion in me to "Go whenever you can!" And my life has been filled with investigating the world, especially my home state of Illinois. At age seven, I recall my mom's car on the ferry that connected two sections of the then-new interstate—I-57—at the Illinois/Kentucky border. At eight, I slept a night in one of the dorms of Southern Illinois University in Carbondale (where my oldest sister was a student); the next morning, my mom took me and my two sisters on a planned vacation. By age 12, I was riding shotgun in my mom's car, reading a map, and directing her where to turn as we traveled here and there.

Fast forward a couple of decades and I was still riding shotgun, still reading the map, but for my husband. From Galena to Cave-in-Rock, we have zigzagged across Illinois countless times over the past three decades.

It's impossible to do justice to such a large state with a checklist of just 100 items. Embedded within many of these pages are extra "tips" that are designed to widen the net as much as possible. With Chicago as the state's largest metropolitan area, there are things listed that pertain to its 77 neighborhoods. However, the Chicagoland area encompasses much more than the city itself or even Cook County. In the suburbs, you'll find limestone bluffs, winding rivers, and the world's largest urban night sky (Palos Preserves). In other regions of the state, you'll find white bison, white horses, and white squirrels.

In Illinois, you'll find some of the nicest people in the world. And in case you think I'm biased, I offer you the words of an older gentleman from South Boston (a "Southie" named Billy), whom I met in fall 2022, during a short hiatus from writing this book. Billy asserted that Midwesterners are the "nicest of all the nation's people." I took his endorsement as the highest form of praise, and share it here.

Three cheers for Midwestern hospitality, ingenuity, and charm! Now, go and find what's fascinating in your backyard, region, state.

Chef Klaus’ Bier Stube, Frankfort

FOOD AND DRINK

1

HOP ABOARD TO DINE
WITH MONTICELLO RAILWAY MUSEUM

Well-traveled train buffs say that Monticello Railway Museum (MRM) is perhaps the best train museum anywhere, but it's MRM's dining excursions that have grabbed attention for more than two decades. On select Saturdays from May through October, you can board a restored Illinois Central dining car for a themed, three-course meal. It could be a Taste of Italy or the Roaring Twenties, but the tickets sell fast (their Polar Express tickets have sold out in 30 minutes), so sign up for their mailing list. MRM also offers monthly Saturday morning "Donut Trains." You'll get to ride in the dining car, and there will be donuts! (Did someone say "donuts"?!)

MRM runs weekend trains between the museum and downtown Monticello, where shops and eateries beckon.

992 Iron Horse Pl., Monticello, 877-762-9011
mrym.org

TIP

Fox River Trolley Museum also runs a Polar Express train (which also sells out fast).

365 S LaFox St., South Elgin, 847-697-4676
foxtrolley.org

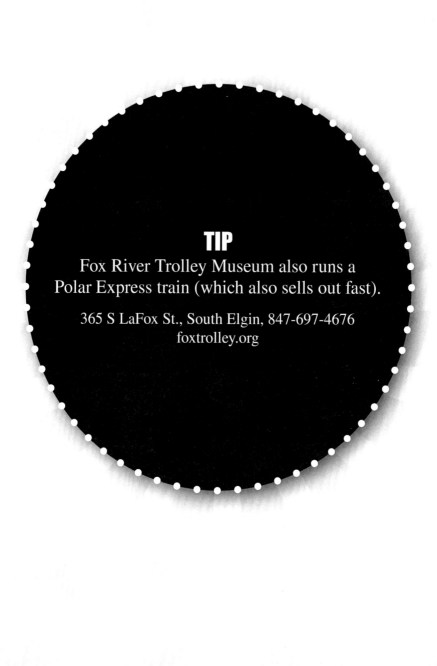

2

DINE WHILE YOU FLOAT
ON LAKE MICHIGAN

The best way to experience Lake Michigan is from a yacht, and in Chicago, an elegant way to do this is by booking a dining cruise with City Experiences (CE)—a company with a fleet for this purpose. With the historic Navy Pier as the launching point, set sail to find breathtaking views of the skyline and enjoy good food, plus DJ entertainment and dancing. CE offers brunch (with bottomless mimosas), lunch, and dinner, and they even offer "Fireworks Dinner Cruises" running from Memorial Day to Labor Day. Lest you think this is only for warm weather, CE offers holiday dinner cruises in December and weekend cruises in January and February. Ahh yes, relax, dine, and float!

600 E Grand Ave., Chicago, 888-957-2634
cityexperiences.com/chicago

TIP

Opt for on-site Navy Pier parking, by reserving in advance at parkabm.com. One option includes up to six hours at a comparatively reasonable price, which gives you time to check out Navy Pier's shops or ride the 200-foot Ferris wheel.

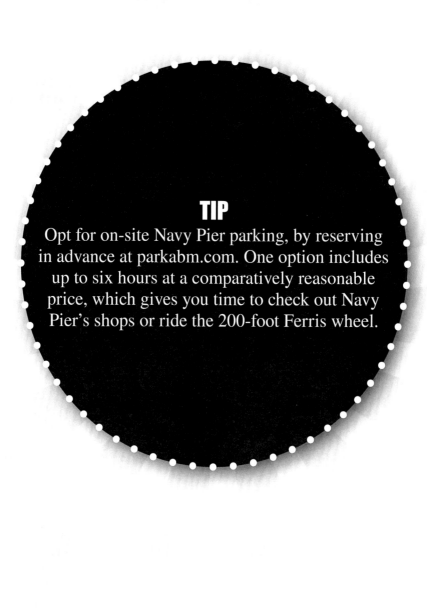

3

ENJOY A CHICAGO-STYLE HOT DOG
AT GENE AND JUDE'S

Their motto says it all: "No Seats. No Ketchup. No Pretense. No Nonsense." No wonder Gene and Jude's has been voted number one in America. If you ask management, they'll tell you the reason they've achieved such high ratings is because their focus is hot dogs and fries. Period. They've been doing it this way since 1946 in the same location. If you go at lunchtime, expect to wait around a half hour, especially weekends. Yes, this means the line is out the door. But the staff handle customers with amazing speed; the person who takes your order gathers your food and gets you to the cash register (sometimes ahead of someone with a larger order). Go for the double-dog; it's inexpensive and worth the wait.

2720 N River Rd., River Grove, 708-452-7634
geneandjudes.com

4

BECOME A WINE CONNOISSEUR

AT AN ILLINOIS WINE EVENT (STATEWIDE)

Illinois has some of the best soil in the world, including that which is required for growing grapes. According to the Sommeliers Choice Awards, "limestone is famous for winemaking," and Illinois has limestone in spades. Wine varieties that love this type of soil include chardonnay, pinot noir, and sauvignon blanc. This means you do not have to go to the Pacific coast for great wine. Tasting rooms abound across Illinois. But what better way to imbibe than to attend a wine festival? Here are some of the state's best offerings.

TIP

If you find yourself in the Wabash Valley wine region, stop in Olney (southeast of Effingham) to see their colony of white squirrels. They're best spotted in spring or fall, early morning (7 to 10 a.m.). Just drive slowly on neighborhood streets around Olney City Park since they hang out around there!

Mackinaw Valley Vineyard in central Illinois holds three (count them!) annual wine festivals, including the International Music, Wine and Craft Brew Fest (late May); Art & Wine Festival (July); and the Grape Stomp & Harvest Festival on the Sunday of Labor Day Weekend. The latter is just what it sounds like—vats full of grapes, and great fun to watch or to participate in the stomping.

33633 State Rt. 9, Mackinaw, 309-359-WINE
mackinawvalleyvineyard.com

Shawnee Hills Wine Trail hosts "Progressive Wine and Food Pairing" events three weekends per year in March, August, and November. One ticket covers 11 wineries, all on the western edge of Shawnee National Forest, from Honker Hill Winery in Carbondale to Alto Vineyard in Alto Pass. The area brims with woodland and lakeside cabins for rent, and there are shuttle services so that all those in your party can imbibe, if desired.

800-248-4373
shawneewinetrail.com/events

Wabash Valley Wine and Art Festival has been held in Palestine for more than 20 years. Located in the valley between the Wabash River (which forms the southeast border of Illinois) and the Little Wabash River (which runs southeast from Mattoon) is a plethora of wineries, most of which show up in the festival in Palestine once a year. A river town, Palestine boasts this festival of wine, art, and food—representing the Wabash Valley region.

618-553-4831
palestinewinefest.com

Not only does the **Mississippi Valley Wine Trail** include the oldest winery in Illinois (in Nauvoo) but the trail also offers multiple annual events. Beginning at the northern tip of the trail in Nauvoo is Baxter's Vineyard, a fifth generation winery. Held Labor Day weekend for over 80 years is the Nauvoo Grape Festival. Baxter's is a vineyard, tasting room, and bed and breakfast, and they make pies from fruit of their own orchards (call ahead if you want it baked or buy it frozen). The rest of the Mississippi Valley Wine Trail includes Press House Winery, on Nauvoo's outskirts; Lake Hill Winery in Carthage; Spirit Knob Winery in Ursa; Village Vineyard in Camp Point; 57 & Vine in Quincy; and Hopewell Winery in Rockport. These seven wineries span just over 80 miles and each offers an array of events—from seafood broils (Hopewell) to "sunset dinners" (57 & Vine). Take that Napa!

800-978-4748
seequincy.com

Summer Wine Fest at Lincoln Park Zoo. This historic world-class zoo, nestled within downtown Chicago, holds a wine tasting event each July, featuring 20 wineries and up to 50 wine varieties. To partake of this experience in a truly unique setting, check their website.

312-742-2000
lpzoo.org/calendar-events

5

EAT A TORNADO
AT SIDNEY DAIRY BARN

The Sidney Dairy Barn's signature freeze treat is the tornado, packed with a storm of flavors, such as Pina Colada, German Chocolate Delight, or the Elvis Tornado (peanut butter, bananas, and marshmallow). If a tornado isn't your thing, try the Dairy Barn's signature Tire Swing—think chocolate chip cookies sandwiching homemade vanilla ice cream and all dunked in chocolate. Be still my heart! In business for almost six decades, this regional institution draws folks from all over east central Illinois (located just 12 miles off of I-57 south of Champaign). Most ice cream shops close in the dead of winter, reopening with fervor come spring, so check the hours before driving far.

311 W Main St., Sidney, 217-688-8026
sidneydairybarn.com

TIP

Other ice cream institutions exist across Illinois, including the Original Rainbow Cone (with various locations, go to the original—big pink—store at 9233 S Western Ave., Chicago), Happy Days Ice Cream Shop (Millstadt; note cash only policy), and Mr. E's Donut & Custard Shop (Belleville)—the latter two are part of the Greater St. Louis region.

6

CRUISE THE MIGHTY MISSISSIPPI ON THE *CELEBRATION BELLE*

Set sail Mark Twain style on the *Celebration Belle*, an 18th century–style paddleboat with narrated lunch cruises and Captain's Dinner-Dances that will take you down the Mississippi River. Lunch and dinner cruises begin as the trees bud out in April, and run through October when those same trees show off their spectacular northern Illinois color. Most cruises vary from an hour and a half to two-and-half hours, though there are "themed" four-hour options once a month (e.g., Broadway tunes, Country hits, etc.), and four-hour Fall Foliage cruises run on October weekends. As November dawns and thoughts turn to the holiday shopping season, give yourself (and loved ones!) a break with a "Holiday Cruise"—held just one day in mid-November. Perhaps it can double as your Thanksgiving family gathering.

2501 River Dr., Moline, 800-297-0034
celebrationbelle.com

7

TEST YOUR WHODUNIT SKILLS
AT A MURDER MYSTERY DINNER (STATEWIDE)

Put your crime-solving finesse to the test by attending a murder mystery dinner, where you can be part of the show. Illinois has several great locations, from big city spots to vineyard or state park backdrops. Fair warning: the criminal might be sitting at your dinner table!

In Chicago, the **Dinner Detective Murder Mystery Dinner Show** is an interactive experience for sleuths young and young-at-heart and includes a prize package for the person who comes closest to cracking the case. Located inside the Marriott-Mag Mile (165 E Ontario St.), Dinner Detective Murder Mystery also performs in Schaumburg, inside the Embassy Suites (1939 Meacham Rd.).

866-496-0535
thedinnerdetective.com

Pere Marquette Lodge in Grafton, near St. Louis, offers themed dinners, including Murder Mystery Dinner Theater during winter months. With a historic lodge as well as cabins and cottages, guests can dine, play, and stay on the edge of 8,000 acres of nature that makes up Pere Marquette State Park.

13653 Lodge Blvd., Grafton, 618-786-2331
pmlodge.net

Mackinaw Valley Vineyard in central Illinois offers murder mystery dinners on a monthly basis from fall through spring. Hands down, their themes are some of the most creative; for example, "We're off to kill the Wizard!" has been a theme for Halloween/October.

33633 State Rt. 9, Mackinaw, 309-359-WINE
mackinawvalleyvineyard.com

Bennett-Curtis House in the village of Grant Park (in Kankakee County) has its own theater group for dinners that take place from fall to spring. This restaurant is inside a turn-of-the-century Victorian home, built in 1900—so much the better for mystery! (P.S. They also offer a Harry Potter–themed dinner.)

302 W Taylor St., Grant Park, 815-465-2288
bennettcurtis.com

EXPERIENCE GERMAN DINING

AT CHEF KLAUS' BIER STUBE

Dining at Chef Klaus' Bier Stube is as authentic as German fare gets in America. With previous iterations in other structures, its current spot in a strip mall belies what's inside—a literal slice of Bavaria. At one end is the "hall," offering live German music on weekends (musical instruments may include cow bells or alpenhorn), in the middle is the fine dining space replete with semi-private nooks, and at the far end is a bar with barfrau or barmann. Once seated, you're greeted by a waitress (wearing dirndl, of course), who bears a breadbasket with two kinds of butter (try the cinnamon) and charcuterie board. For entrée, you'll find sauerbraten (beef), hähnchenbrust (chicken), lamb, duck, seafood, and 13 kinds of schnitzel. Then choose the accompaniments (including liver dumpling soup, spaetzle, red cabbage, etc.). With steins of all sizes lining the walls, plus cuckoo clocks and all manner of German artifacts, those who have dined at Klaus' table for decades use it to measure all other German dining.

20827 S LaGrange Ave., Frankfort, 815-469-0940
chefklausgermanrestaurants.com

9

FIND THE BEST CHICKEN IN THE MIDWEST

AT WHITE FENCE FARM

A Midwest institution for "Chicken Dinners" since the 1920s, White Fence Farm promises perfection. With just one sit-down restaurant that is open for dinner only (4–8 p.m.), Tuesday through Saturday, and noon to 8 p.m. on Sundays, carry-out locations were added to meet public demand (Joliet, Downers Grove, Riverside). But you need to go to the main restaurant to see the animals. In their lobby, you'll be greeted by a mish-mosh of antique cars, snow globes, typewriters, and other fun stuff. Once you're seated and dinner comes, you'll feast on four pieces of fried-to-perfection chicken, corn fritters, cole slaw, and your choice of fries or mashed potatoes (for the ultimate in comfort food, go for mashed). Afterward, visit their alpacas and Norwegian Dwarf goats across the parking lot, behind the white fence. This family-owned restaurant has stood the test of time for very good reasons. It's an absolute must for chicken lovers. You're welcome!

1376 Joliet Rd., Romeoville, 630-739-1720
whitefencefarm-il.com

10

ENJOY THE BEST OF SOUL FOOD

AT NEIL ST. BLUES

When owner Gayle Starkes decided to open a restaurant, she envisioned a place for family. Using her grandmother's recipes, and with her kids and extended family members pitching in now and then, she has created something truly special—a soul food restaurant with New Orleans Cajun flair. Starkes says, "When it comes to soul food, it's all about the sides." At Neil St. Blues, they offer a plethora of side dishes to go with your fried catfish or vegan jambalaya, including a candied yam dish like grandma used to make.

True to their musical name, Neil St. Blues offers live music when possible. One thing Starkes believes is that the world needs more dancing. So, when you visit, and if there's music, don't be shy. Let the beat take you. Then sit back down for dessert. Southern-style banana pudding or peach cobbler, anyone?

301 N Neil St., Champaign, 217-531-1150
neilstblues.com

MORE SOUL FOOD SPOTS

MacArthur's Restaurant has served many celebrities, including Oprah and President Obama. Located on Chicago's west side (Austin neighborhood).

5412 W Madison, Chicago, 773-261-2316

Hidden Manna Cafe has been serving Cajun and Southern-style dishes to pleased customers for two decades, and has been featured on WGN-TV's "Chicago's Best." They source fresh ingredients from local suppliers.

3613 216th St., Matteson, 708-248-5571

Oooh Wee! It is! is a restaurant where they promise that you'll say their name—with enthusiasm—when you taste their food. Their original location at 2208 E State St. in Burnham is take-away only, but it's their second place that is a hot spot to dine-in. The interior is splashed with art, color, and fun. And the food, oh the food!

33 E 83rd St., Chicago, 872-244-7505
ooohweeitis.org

VISIT A WORKING FARM

AND THEN EAT THEIR FOOD AT EPIPHANY FARMS RESTAURANT

Epiphany Farms has it all. They have a solid ethos of running a sustainable farm-to-table business while educating the public about what they do. They serve their own grown vegetables, meat, and eggs. And they've grown from one restaurant to three during their first decade. They run "Anju Above" upstairs from their flagship Epiphany Farms Restaurant, and they also operate a Korean barbecue. Their main restaurant offers steak, seafood, Yuba (tofu pocket stuffed with pickled veggies and rice), butternut squash conchas (Mexican sweet bread), and more. So much more. They list nine allergies for guests to check off the list so that these "CheFarmers" can take care with sensitive patrons. Tours of their farm in Downs occur seasonally. Thank goodness for Earth-conscious, energetic folks!

220 E Front St., Bloomington, 309-828-2323
epiphanyfarms.com

TIP

Farther downstate, Firefly Grill in Effingham is another restaurant that offers farm-to-table food; their co-founder and chef, Niall Campbell, was named "Best Chef" by culinary peers. Located near the crossroads of I-57 and I-70, Firefly offers eclectic ambience and pet-friendly spaces on their porch.

12

FIND 90 FLAVORS OF CHEESECAKE

AT TRIPLE DIPPLE'S IN CHILLICOTHE

Triple Dipple's does one thing and they do it so well that they've earned "Best Dessert" accolades back-to-back at Taste of Peoria. And that's just since they opened in 2017 and before the pandemic caused festival cancellations. Inside Triple Dipple's store in downtown Chillicothe, it's all cheesecake, all day long, either full size or mini/personal pan size. Away from the store, they're in their "Cheesecake Chariot," the food truck that takes them to festivals and markets around the greater Peoria region and beyond.

When asked to make something other than one of their 90 cheesecake flavors, Triple Dipple's owner and chief baker, Harreld Webster Jr., caters fruit pizza, sandwiches, and various other sweets, including handmade chocolate lollipops. But on National Cheesecake Day, celebrated on July 30 each year (mark your calendar!), choose that sweet custard-in-a-tart in one of Webster's signature flavors. There's Root Beer Float Cheesecake, Raspberry White Chocolate Cookie Dough, and come fall harvest time, line up for Apple Cider Cheesecake. Whose mouth is watering right now?

940 N 2nd St., Chillicothe, 309-340-9540
tripledipples.com

13

EAT DEEP DISH PIZZA
WHERE IT WAS INVENTED (STATEWIDE)

Just as Naples, Italy, lays claim to the birthplace of pizza, Chicago bore the deep dish version of the pizza pie. It was during the 1940s that a young Lou Malnati worked in Chicago's "first deep dish pizzeria." Malnati later took his skills, and with his wife, opened a restaurant in the Chicago suburb of Lincolnwood. There, business boomed, and they have added more locations over the ensuing 50+ years. At this writing, there are 60 locations of Lou Manalti's Pizzeria in northeast Illinois. A fascinating find is their "Ship a Pizza" option to enjoy nationwide. With a crust that is more like a layer of bread, deep dish pizza will slow down your fastest eaters. It takes about 40 minutes to cook a deep dish, so, be prepared to make it a true dining experience. That is, after all, the Italian way!

Use Malnati's "location finder" atloumalnatis.com/chicagoland

MORE PIZZA PLACES ACROSS THE STATE THAT RANK HIGH ON THE LISTS OF ILLINOIS FOODIES

Vito and Nick's Pizzeria
8433 S Pulaski, Chicago

Monical's Pizza has 40+ locations spread across central and eastern Illinois, as far northwest as Princeton, and as far south as Centralia.

Walt's Pizza, where their Double Decker is to die for—it's not on their online menu but they make it!

213 S Court St., Marion, 618-993-8668
waltspizza.com

Quatro's Deep Pan Pizza, order their deep dish deluxe (you'll thank me later).

218 W Freeman St., Carbondale, 618-549-5326
quatros.com

14

TASTE A NEW BREW
AT A CRAFT BREWFEST (STATEWIDE)

The brewing of craft beers has exploded in popularity over recent years, and an outcrop of that phenomenon is the prevalence of brewfests. Whether you've attempted homebrewing techniques or you're so serious as to have taken a class on perfecting grain-to-glass skills, attending a craft brewfest is a must for any aficionado of this brewed beverage. On the following page, you'll find some of the best brewfests in the state. Some include barbecue and others have fantastic music. Whatever your taste or mood, there's one for you.

Big Muddy Monster Brewfest in Murphysboro marks its 13th year in 2023, and has become a highly anticipated event in southern Illinois. Located along the Big Muddy River, near Carbondale, the Murphysboro brewfest is held in early October and draws breweries from across the Midwest.

Murphysboro Chamber of Commerce, 618-684-6421
bmmbrewfest.com

'Que and Brew offers a "Pro and Backyard BBQ Competition" as well as 40+ craft beers and cocktails. Held in Edwardsville, a stone's throw from St. Louis, this festival takes place each October.

edwqueandbrew.com

Pretzel City Brewfest, held in Freeport each September. Known for a historic bakery that once made famous pretzels, Freeport is just 35 minutes west of Rockford.

815-233-1350, greaterfreeport.com/visit/events

Zoo Brew at Brookfield Zoo has been held annually for more than a decade. Held in mid to late summer, this festival is held on zoo grounds where you just might hear a lion roar or a wolf howl while you're checking out up to 80 brews.

czs.org/events

Devon on Tap: Decatur Craft Beer and Music Festival is a collaboration between the Decatur Area Arts Council and the Decatur Parks Foundation, held at the Devon Lakeshore Amphitheater along beautiful Lake Decatur.

2686 E Cantrell St., Decatur, 217-423-3189
decaturarts.org

Brüegala/BOOgala! A brew fest with a Halloween theme! Hosted by Bloomington-Normal Jaycees on a Friday evening in October for the past 20+ years, you'll find local breweries, food vendors, and live bands. Held at Courthouse Square.

McLean County Courthouse
104 W Front St., Bloomington
bruegala.com

Paddlewheel Riverboat
on the Fox River, St. Charles

MUSIC AND ENTERTAINMENT

15

CHECK OUT

THE ONLY EGYPTIAN THEATRE EAST OF THE ROCKIES

West of the Rockies, you'll find Grauman's Egyptian Theatre on Hollywood Boulevard in Los Angeles. East of the Rockies, smack dab in northeast Illinois, is the Midwest's very own Egyptian Theatre in DeKalb. More than 100 similarly styled theaters were built around the country following the 1922 discovery of King Tut's tomb, when all things Egyptian peaked in the 1920s and '30s. Today, DeKalb's Egyptian Theatre is one of just five that remain. Thanks to citizens who saved it from the wrecking ball, it's a venue that offers concerts, Ragtime Orchestra, and the Nutcracker ballet at Christmastime. When you go, notice the smaller elements that complete the Egyptian theme, including a carving of King Tut above Exit signs (look closely).

135 N 2nd St., DeKalb, 815-758-1215
egyptiantheatre.org

TIP

Northern Illinois University (NIU) is just down the road from the theater, which means you can make a day of your trip to DeKalb by walking NIU's nature trail along the South Branch Kishwaukee River and visiting their Art Museum at Artgeld Hall.

SEE THE WORLD'S LARGEST MAILBOX
AND OTHER BIG THINGS

Some states tout big balls of twine, but in Casey, there are 23 BIG attractions, including several "World's Largest" items, as certified by Guinness. There's a windchime, mailbox, rocking chair, barbershop pole, people-sized birdcage, the list goes on. Not only are these BIG things fun to see—and free—but posing with them produces unique pictures your friends won't believe. Where else can you climb inside of a mailbox? The funniest photo op comes from posing in front of the BIG antlers. Located just off I-70, Casey can brighten anyone's day. And since this little town has been playing host to curious visitors for over 10 years (ever since Jim Bolin put up the first BIG attraction), amenities are convenient (clean restrooms are by the mailbox).

Main St. and Central Ave., Casey
bigthingssmalltown.com

TIP

For extra special lodging in Casey, Eighteen-Ninety Sleepover is in downtown near all the BIG action. A renovated 1890 structure with modern charm. Pssst: One of their rooms has a Gryffindor theme. eighteen-ninetysleepover.com.

TOUR WOODSTOCK,
HOME OF ORSON WELLES AND *GROUNDHOG DAY*

Woodstock is a place right out of the movies—literally. Its town square was the backdrop for the 1993 film *Groundhog Day*, with Bill Murray awaking in the same town, over and over. The Woodstock Mural, located in a pedway off Main Street, depicts scenes from the movie, as well as highlights other big names who got their start in this town.

A teenage Orson Welles learned much of his craft at Woodstock Opera House. Later, Paul Newman honed his acting chops on the opera house stage—all while working day jobs in local shops. Today, this "Grand Capitol of Midwestern Victorianism," as Welles called the opera house, offers brass bands, ballet, and musicals such as Rodgers & Hammerstein's *Cinderella*.

Woodstock is a well-preserved example of the way that many towns were laid out in the 18th century, with the town square in the middle, and shops and theaters encircling the square. One can almost hear the town crier, shouting the news to citizens.

121 Van Buren St., Woodstock, 815-338-5300
woodstockoperahouse.com

WATCH THE WORLD-FAMOUS
DANCING LIPIZZAN HORSES

Tempel Farm has been raising Lipizzan horses since the family's patriarch/matriarch saw them perform in Vienna in the late 1950s. Lipizzans are a rare breed of white stallion, originally bred for royalty in the 16th century—the Hapsburg royal family of Austria to be exact. The centuries-long careful breeding of Lipizzans brings a horse born with the genetic material to perform graceful moves to music, which we call dancing. At Tempel Farm, they call it an "expression of harmony through movement." When you see Lipizzans sashay to classical music, you will call it . . . stunning! Temple Farm offers a summer line-up of performances, plus holiday performances on two Saturdays in December. You could fly to Austria to see Lipizzans, where they've performed for 450 years. Or you can see them at Tempel Farm, where these legendary stallions have been exhibited since 1982. Tempel's Lipizzan herd is now the largest in the world, and they're the only one in the nation doing what they do. Prepare yourself to fall in love!

17000 Wadsworth Rd., Old Mill Creek, 847-244-5330
tempelfarms.com

19

GET A THREEFER
AT CHICAGO'S MUSEUM CAMPUS

Hit three preeminent venues by visiting Chicago's Museum Campus. The Field Museum, one of the elite museums of the nation, is mere steps from the Shedd Aquarium. And a short walk from the Shedd is Adler Planetarium. Which means one visit can mean a winning trifecta! At the Field, you can go "Inside Ancient Egypt," plus see SUE T.rex and the Tsavo Lions. Adults: Watch the movie before seeing the lions! At Shedd Aquarium are beluga whales, sea lions, and octopi (oh my!), all in a structure that retains its original 1930 octagonal shape. At the Adler, the first planetarium in the Western hemisphere to open to the public, visitors connect with the cosmic neighborhood in the sky through shows and exhibits. Perhaps you'll visit Pluto, join a Space Express Tour of the solar system in the year 2096, or learn about the moon from Big Bird. Adler's shows take place in their iconic dome theater and are updated as science makes new discoveries. The city of Chicago offers the "City Pass," which includes five institutions including these three.

Field Museum
1400 S DuSable Lake Shore Dr., Chicago, 312-922-9410
fieldmuseum.org

Shedd Aquarium
1200 S DuSable Lake Shore Dr.
Chicago, 312-939-2438
sheddaquarium.org

Adler Planetarium
1300 S DuSable Lake Shore Dr.
Chicago, 312-922-7827
adlerplanetarium.org

TIP

Metra Electric train has a Museum Campus stop that stops at Michigan Avenue at 11th Street, about a 10-minute walk to the campus. Use the pedestrian bridge over the railroad tracks, cross Columbus Drive, and then take the tunnel under DuSable Lake Shore Drive. If you drive, park at Soldier Field-North Garage, 1452 Special Olympics Drive.

RIDE HIGH
ON AERIE'S SKYTOUR

The confluence of the Mississippi and Illinois rivers is a stunning sight, and the best way to see it is from 300 feet up in the air via the SkyTour operated by Aerie's Resort. At the Landings at Aerie's, you'll choose an open-air chair or an enclosed gondola cabin. Your ride takes you to the top of the bluff, atop which sits Aerie's Resort, including a winery and restaurant. (Note that the SkyTour is the only way to get to the restaurant unless you're an Aerie's lodging guest. Being on a bluff does not allow for parking expansion despite rising popularity.)

Also atop Aerie's bluff is the Alpine Coaster, newly opened in fall 2022. This gravity coaster operates year-round, making Aerie's a great destination in cold weather. You could spend hours (or the night) at Aerie's, or you may decide to SkyTour it to the top, soak up the views, then coaster it (or SkyTour it) back to the bottom.

The Landings at Aerie's
14 W Main St., Grafton, 618-786-8439
aeriesresort.com

ENJOY MUSIC WITH A VIEW
AT CHICAGO'S NORTHERLY ISLAND

Imagine yourself watching your favorite band. Now envision the backdrop to that band is a magnificent city skyline, with Lake Michigan draped nearby. As the sun sets, the city lights flicker on and add to your view. That's the experience of attending a concert on Northerly Island, a man-made peninsula that was originally a municipal airport (closed after 9-11). Northerly Island now touts a nature path, bike trail, and the outdoor amphitheater for concerts, called "Huntington Bank Pavilion at Northerly Island." Opened in 2005, this outdoor concert venue is a warm-weather attraction. Run by the Chicago Park District, Northerly Island is part of Chicago's Museum Campus. It's best to park at Soldier Field-North Garage (1452 Special Olympics Dr.), and then walk east along Solidarity Drive toward the planetarium; the entrance to the Pavilion is from Solidarity Drive just before you reach the planetarium.

1300 S Linn White Dr., Chicago
For concert listings, call 312-540-2668 or go topavilionnortherlyisland.com

Chicago Park District can be reached at 312-742-PLAY

22

BE A STEAM ENGINEER
AT THE ILLINOIS RAILWAY MUSEUM

If you've dreamed of being at the throttle of a full-size steam locomotive, the Illinois Railway Museum (IRM) is the place for you. For those 18 or older, reserve a 25-minute time slot on one of the two designated Steam Engineer Days per year. Opened in 1964, IRM is home to the largest collection of historic railway equipment in America, and has grown into a train lover's dream come true, with 100 acres of opportunities. You can ride an authentic Interurban train to IRM's pumpkin patch in the fall, or catch the "Bunny Hop Trolley" to the "carrot patch" come spring. If you're looking to book an autumn- or Christmas-themed ride, they offer these, too. Open from late April to late October, there's literally something for every train lover out there.

7000 Olson Rd., Union, 815-923-4000
irm.org

SEE THE WORLD-FAMOUS VOLO AUTO MUSEUM

With seven miles of exhibits, Volo Auto Museum began in car sales—with vintage autos offered for sale. The autos drew such a crowd of inquisitive folks that the owners eventually added "museum" to their name and charged admission. Five decades later, they still sell cars. Not just vintage—some sell for six figures! Ever wonder where Hollywood gets those great cars for TV or movies? Or where those cars end up when the filming is done? You can find some answers at Volo. Here, you'll see "Christine" (Stephen King's baby), Eleanor Mustang (*Gone in 60 Seconds*), Greased Lightning (*Grease*), "Ecto-1" (*Ghostbusters*), the eye-catching Batmobile, and the list goes on. There are Duesenbergs, vintage RVs (one with a pot belly stove!), celebrity guitars, vintage bicycles, scooters, and toys. Even Volo's on-site pizza parlor is a veritable museum. Volo is open daily and is fun for kids. Just be sure to wear comfortable walking shoes, and bring a stroller for tiny tykes who might tucker out after a mile or two of ambling.

27582 Volo Village Rd., Volo, 815-385-3644
volocars.com

24

SLEEP IN A HISTORIC MANSION

AT ALLERTON PARK AND RETREAT CENTER

Allerton is 1,500 acres of bliss. Its story began in 1900 when it was built by artist and philanthropist Robert Allerton, a frequent traveler who furnished his estate with art from around the world. In 1946, he donated his home and grounds to the University of Illinois, and it's now operated by university staff as a park, event space, and lodging destination.

The mansion offers 17 guest rooms, plus there's lodging in its outbuildings. Formal gardens beckon guests, including a Chinese maze garden, sunken garden, and walled garden—all with exquisite statuary. The park is open to the public from 8 a.m. to sunset, and includes 14 miles of hiking trails through Allerton Woods. With all of this, you'll surely find serenity. Staying at Allerton requires you to pack in your own food and beverages, since the on-site café is seasonal; when open, its hours are 10 a.m. to 4 p.m. However, staff will make coffee early in the morning, and if there's coffee, we can survive! Besides lodging, Allerton offers concerts, guided hikes, and movie nights. You really must see it to believe it.

515 Old Timber Rd., Monticello, 217-333-3287
allerton.illinois.edu

TIP

Stay when the flower gardens are in full bloom. Also, ask about their "glamping package," which includes a bonfire and s'mores (seasonal). Note that some, but not all, of their rooms have a microwave; if you need access to one, ask the staff.

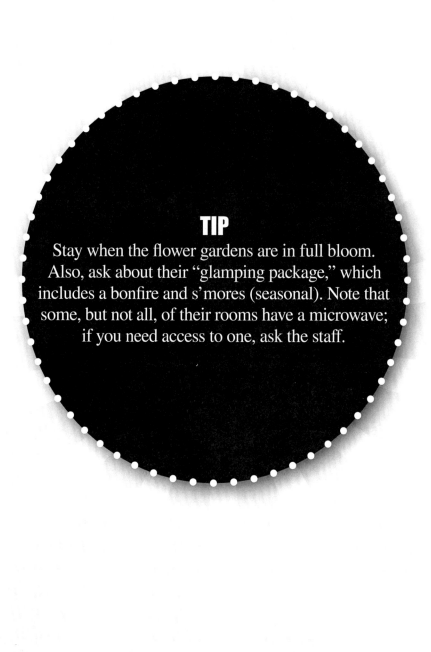

PLAY ALL DAY

AND THEN SLEEP IN A CABOOSE AT WILDLIFE PRAIRIE PARK

Imagine sleeping in a vintage caboose, comfortable and clean, complete with bed, couch, and kitchen, and you look out the window and see bison or elk in the distance. Sound like a dream? Well, wake up, because this dream can come true at the historical Wildlife Prairie Park (WPP). By day, you can walk among WPP's bears and cougars, board their train, grab lunch, and perhaps rent a kayak. Later, check into your (pre-registered) lodging. Pssst, they also have horse stables that house overnight guests. There are enough lodging options here for a family reunion or just a cozy couple's getaway. Voted "Best Hidden Gem" by *Peoria Magazine*, this place is a true treasure.

3826 N Taylor Rd., Hanna City, 309-676-0998
wildlifeprairiepark.org

TIP

WPP is just 20 minutes from Peoria Riverfront Museum, a unique multidisciplinary museum (combining art, science, history, and achievement), and it also has a planetarium. Beam me up, Scotty, I'm ready to go!

VISIT SUPERMAN'S HOMETOWN OF METROPOLIS

That's right. The man of steel "hails" from a town at the southern tip of Illinois. And the 15-foot Superman statue in the town square proves it! The Super Museum, with its collection of more than 70,000 items, also offers "super" gifts and clothing. Two blocks north of the museum is a statue of Lois Lane holding her pen and paper. If you visit the second weekend in June, you'll catch "Superman Celebration," which includes comic artists, celebrities, food, and memorabilia. So, get your geek on, and maybe a costume, and join the crowd! Note that Metropolis upgraded their parking in 2022 with a new big (free) parking lot at 6th and Pearl Streets. Attending Superman weekend requires that you book lodging way in advance (check supermancelebration.net).

The Superman statue is near the Superman Museum
517 Market St., Metropolis, 618-524-5518
supermuseum.com

TIP

Also in Metropolis is Fort Massac State Park, with a replica colonial fort, visitor center, camping, fishing, hiking, and boating. Each October is Fort Massac Encampment, when history comes alive.

1308 E 5th St., Metropolis, 618-524-4712
www2.illinois.gov/dnr

VISIT THE WORLD-CLASS
BROOKFIELD ZOO

Brookfield Zoo (BZ) is more than lions, tigers, and bears. At its Tropic World exhibit, you can find primates in what was built as the largest zoo exhibit building in the world when it opened in 1982. Simulated rain falls hourly (on the half-hour) on the primates, at which time they run for cover; when the rain ends, they come back out. This form of behavioral enrichment is good for them and fun to watch. BZ's Great Bear Wilderness features bison, too, with a tunnel for visitors to traverse, with bison able to roam overhead. From giraffe feedings to the world-class Hamill Family Play Zoo, a trip to this zoo is a must. If your last trip was years ago, it's time to see what's new (besides the new CEO who took the helm in 2022).

3300 Golf Rd., Brookfield, 708-688-8000
czs.org

TIP

Brookfield Zoo's north/main gate parking is large, connected to the zoo by a tunnel under 31st Street. The south gate is much smaller but perfect in cold weather since there are fewer steps to the entrance. Also, winter is a great time to see their giraffes when they're housed indoors (visitors get oh-so-close!).

ENJOY A PADDLEWHEEL RIVERBOAT

ON THE FOX RIVER

St. Charles has touted paddlewheel excursions since the 1940s, thanks to a family-owned operation. When the owners retired in 2018, the St. Charles Park District secured the operation, and now runs this charming, 1800s-style transport. From May to October, narrated cruises begin near the heart of downtown and journey along the Fox River's deepest section of its 200-mile path through Illinois. Along which, shadows of Al Capone flicker (yes, he hid out here) and nesting eagles flock to the preserves along the Fox. Also, one of their two boats can be rented for private excursions, which conjures visions of a riverboat birthday bash. With themed cruises aimed at families as well as excursions for 21 and up, this experience can soothe even the wildest beast.

8 North Ave., St. Charles, 630-584-2334
stcriverboats.com

TIP

Walk the riverside trail south from the boat dock to Collins Tower, and climb it for a birds-eye view. Then, walk a bit farther south to the "Potawatomi Indian" statue; its inscription speaks of the people who once lived here.

29

SEE STARS BEFORE THEY BECOME FAMOUS AT SECOND CITY COMEDY CLUB

When you walk into Second City Comedy Club's (SCCC) entrance hallway, 60 years of history line the walls. Stars who have appeared here before making it big include Joan Rivers, John Candy, Gilda Radner, John Belushi, Dan Akroyd, Keegan-Michael Key, Valerie Harper, Bonnie Hunt, Steven Colbert, and the list goes on. The trick is to save your Stagebill. Tuck it away someplace safe, and every five years or so, review the faces of those you saw. Eventually, you'll recognize at least one name, probably more. If you've never been to SCCC's Mainstage, this is where you start. Later, perhaps you can hit their e.t.c. Theater. Located in Chicago's Old Town neighborhood, street parking is scarce; use the parking garage next door to the club.

Mainstage
1616 N Wells St., 2nd Floor, Chicago

e.t.c. Theater
230 W North Ave., Chicago
312-337-3992, secondcity.com

TIP

If you want to stack up your comedy delights, another historic comedy club, Zanie's Comedy Night Club, is a block south of SCCC. A different set-up and vibe, but with tons of laughs. chicago.zanies.com

30

ENJOY CHICAGO'S OLDEST FREE FESTIVAL,

THE JAZZ FESTIVAL

When Duke Ellington died in 1974, musicians cried. And Chicago held its first jazz festival. Held on Labor Day weekend, the festival is based mainly at Millennium Park, which runs along Michigan Avenue in downtown Chicago, and also includes other nearby stages, including one at the Chicago Cultural Center. Whether you find a chair or patch of grass and stay for one performance or wander around all day (or multiple days), some of the best talent in jazz is found at this annual festival. Hosted by the City of Chicago's Office of Cultural Affairs & Special Events, this spectacular event is one that every jazz lover should attend.

Millennium Park
201 E Randolph, Chicago, 312-744-5000
chicago.gov

ATTEND THE ILLINOIS STATE FAIR

AND DISCOVER THE "ROUTE 66 EXPERIENCE"

Celebrate Illinois at the State Fair, where you'll find live music, livestock, racing, food, carnival fun, and a life-size "butter cow" sculpted completely of, well, butter. An icon of the fair since the 1920s, the butter cow dwells in the dairy building. New to the fairgrounds in summer 2022 was the Giant Slide, positioned so that patrons can "slide down Route 66." For 2023, a bigger bolder exhibit will open, called the Route 66 Experience. Utilizing the one-acre space on the southeast corner of the fairgrounds, the Experience is a year-round, self-guided, immersive exhibit, including walk-through huts, or "time capsules," each highlighting a decade of Illinois history. Curation of these time capsules has been spearheaded by the Route 66 Scenic Byway, along with the communities highlighted in the capsules. Route 66 winds its way through 400 miles of Illinois and about 90 communities, and the Experience memorializes all of it—what a treat!

801 E Sangamon Ave., Springfield, 217-782-6661
www2.illinois.gov/statefair

TIP

Illinois has had two state fairs since 1986 when then-governor Jim Thompson bought a private fair in downstate DuQuoin. Though much smaller, DuQuoin State Fair offers harness races, rodeos, and other state fair–type activities.

618-542-1515
www2.illinois.gov/sites/dsf/pages/default.aspx

32

SEE A MOVIE
AT A DRIVE-IN THEATER (STATEWIDE)

Nothing says America like a drive-in movie—or at least that used to be the case. At the height of its popularity, the US had 4,000 of these theaters. Approximately 300 remain, and less than a dozen of them are in Illinois. If you've never sat in your car with a speaker hanging off your window to pipe in movie dialogue as you stare through your windshield at a huge screen at the front of the parking lot in which you sit, you must do it. This experience is part of American culture and it's slowly disappearing. Your choice will be geographically dependent unless you're on a road trip. Luckily, there are several to choose from.

Central—Route 66 Drive-In

1700 Knights Recreation Dr., Springfield, 217-698-0066
route66-drivein.com

South central—Litchfield Skyview Drive-In

1500 N Historic Route 66, Litchfield, 217-324-4451
litchfieldskyview.com

St. Louis area—Belleville Skyview Drive-In Movie Theater

5700 N Belt W, Belleville, 618-233-4400
skyview-drive-in.com

North central—Route 34 Drive-In

Cash only.

4468 E 12th Rd., Earlville (LaSalle County), 815-246-9700
rt34drivein.com

Northwest—Midway Drive-In and Diner

91 Palmyra Rd., Sterling, 847-647-3124
themidwaydrivein.net

East central—Fairview Drive 'N Theatre

16045 E Hwy. 33, Newton, 618-455-3100
driventheatre.com

GO OUT ON THE GLASS LEDGE

AT WILLIS TOWER

If you want a high-in-the-sky experience, the Glass Ledge at Chicago's Willis Tower is for you. First, the facts. Willis Tower (former Sears Tower) is the second-tallest building in the Western Hemisphere (or the tallest, depending on whether antennas are counted). Opened in 2009, the Ledge is a see-through glass observation deck, basically a box, that extends out from the 103rd floor of Willis Tower's Skydeck—1,353 feet from the ground. On a clear day, you can see four states. Photos taken of you inside the Ledge look as though you're floating above Chicago, and you just might feel like it. For the best views, arrive soon after the Skydeck opens.

233 S Wacker Dr., Chicago, but use Franklin or Jackson St. entrance
312-875-9447
theskydeck.com

TIP

The Metra station closest to Willis Tower is Union Station (Metra and Amtrak). If you're seeing other downtown attractions, check out the City Pass to save some cash.

GROOVE TO TUNES
AT RAVINIA FESTIVAL

Billed as the oldest and most programmatically diverse music festival in North America, Ravinia Festival has been a tradition since 1904. Lasting all summer, Ravinia hosts an array of musicians; past names include Yo-Yo Ma and Dolly Parton. Though Ravinia's reputation is as an outdoor venue, they have a pavilion with reserved seating. In the grass, however, is where it's at, since food and drink are welcome on the lawn, including alcohol for those of age. Some attendees are known to set up tiny tables, LED candles, and break out wine glasses as they lounge in bag chairs. As the food and drink fuse with the sound of music and crickets, and a child totters nearby with a smile and a wave, this is when you realize why Ravinia is one of the most enchanting music festivals in the nation.

Lawn seats are not within view of the pavilion stage, but you can walk up and get a look anytime. If the performance is one you must watch in its entirety, go for reserved seating. And always (always) arrive early.

201 Ravinia Park Rd., Highland Park, 847-266-5100
ravinia.org

MAKE IT ALL ABOUT FAMILY, FOOD, AND FUN

AT ECKERT'S FARM

Eight generations of Eckerts have made their Belleville farm a special place for families. "Whatever family means to you, we're here to help you make memories," say the Eckerts. Their Belleville Country Restaurant serves chicken and dumplings so good that "grandma is our only competition." (They sell dumplings by the quart to-go!) The vegetables and fruit that grace their menu mostly come from their farms, which they open to the public during harvest for U-Pick experiences. A bounty of apple and peach trees and pumpkin patches await guests to pick and play come fall. And come Christmastime, Eckert's Farm offers wagon rides to families who want to chop their own tree (or pick a pre-cut one). From the first fruit of the season (strawberries) in May, to the pumpkins of fall, and Christmas trees, Eckert's is the place for families of two, five, ten, or more! Eckert's also has some U-Pick options (seasonally) at their Millstadt and Grafton farms.

951 S Green Mount Rd., Belleville, 618-233-0513
eckerts.com

RIDE 15 ROLLERCOASTERS
AT SIX FLAGS GREAT AMERICA

That's right, Great America has 15 rollercoasters, making it a favorite among adrenaline junkies. It's also DC Heaven. As in, DC Comic characters. There's Batman: The Ride, where you'll fly like the dark knight, with your feet dangling as you hurl through a zero-gravity spin. Other DC coasters include Superman: Ultimate Flight and The Joker: Free-Fly Coaster. Need more? There's more! Looney Tunes characters call Great America home as well, so you can expect to see Bugs Bunny around the park. And the stage shows are so very good. One thing to keep in mind is that Six Flags built Hurricane Harbor next door, but they're separate parks. This means you'll want to consider this when you're choosing your admission pass. You might want to buy a two-day pass and stay overnight in the area. Buying your pass in advance is a MUST. Parking is cheaper when combined with your pass purchase. Also, you can "add-on" a meal package with your admission pass. There are many options. Weigh each one according to your needs/wants.

1 Great America Pkwy., Gurnee, 847-249-1776
sixflags.com/greatamerica

SEE A LIVE SHOW
AT THE HISTORIC CHICAGO THEATRE

The Chicago Theatre's vertical sign on State Street is a beloved symbol of the city, but it's what's inside that you need to see. Opened in 1921, the theater set the standard for movie palaces across America. Called the "Wonder Theater of the World," its lavish design includes a mini replica of Paris's Arc de Triomphe (six stories high) above its marquee, a grand staircase modeled after the Paris Opera House, and a grand lobby modeled after the Royal Chapel in Versailles. And that's all before you reach your seat. Today, the theater touts some of the hottest tickets in live music, comedy, and even a FLOTUS (First Lady of the US) now and then (Michelle Obama, December 2022). If you haven't been to this theater, you must.

175 N State St., Chicago, 312-462-6300
msg.com/the-chicago-theatre

TIP

Chicago also has "Broadway in Chicago," comprised of five theaters.
broadwayinchicago.com

VISIT GOLDMAN-KUENZ SCULPTURE PARK

AT CEDARHURST CENTER FOR THE ARTS

Cedarhurst takes art and education seriously. A cultural mecca of sorts, it consists of an art museum, music performance hall, historical homes, and the Goldman-Kuenz Sculpture Park. The latter has grown to one of the largest outdoor contemporary sculpture collections in the United States, with 73 pieces spread out over 80 acres. One of the earliest sculptures commissioned for the park is Kimball the horse; made of old automobile hubcaps, he's a visitor favorite. Featuring the work of career artists alongside emerging artists, many mediums are used in the sculptures, including steel, stone, and even concrete. This oasis of art is set in a small town, making it all the more special.

2600 Richview Rd., Mount Vernon, 618-242-1236
cedarhurst.org

TIP

If you can, visit when Cedarhurst's music series occurs (two performances in spring, two in fall). A win-win!

39

SPEND UP TO 24 HOURS
AT KING SPA & SAUNA

A spa that charges one admission price for up to 24 hours sounds too good to be true. But it's not. Since 2010, King Spa & Sauna has offered ancient Asian treatments in a setting so unique that it's culture-bending. Here, you'll find a patented sauna (infused with siraka) that's offered in only three places worldwide. Full disclosure: there's a nude policy in the wet spa area, where your toxins are washed away before entering the inner sanctum. You can request a private shower, but for the real Korean bath experience, do as the Romans do—folks of all ages and shapes strip down. After cleansing, you'll don a uniform (provided to you) and enter the area with themed saunas. One is the Pyramid Room, infused with 23 karat gold (gold purifies!). The saunas are included in your admission fee. Other services cost extra, including acupressure or massages. King Spa is open 24/7, and no reservation is required, which means you can decide any time, any hour, to pursue Korean-style healing.

809 Civic Center Dr., Niles, 847-972-2540
kingspa.com

TIP

H-Mart, a big Korean grocery store, is in the same shopping complex as King Spa. If you've been searching for Nori Maki Arare (rice crackers with seaweed), they have it.

hmart.com

SEE WHY BLUE MAN GROUP HAS DAZZLED AUDIENCES FOR 25+ YEARS

Blue Man Group is one of those experiences that escapes description. Are they comedians? Yes. Do they make music? Yep. Do they combine beautiful colors and mediums to create art? Sure do. And yet, there's no one else like them. Though they perform on the East Coast and in Vegas, and they've performed in Berlin, it is Chicago's Briar Street Theatre that they've called home for more than 25 years. The magic begins as soon as you're seated, as you begin hearing stories about the people around (or with) you. During the show, if you're in the front row, you might be invited on stage. Go with it if you're able. People come from all over the Midwest to Chicago's Briar Street Theatre. You should, too.

3133 N Halsted St., Chicago, 800-BLUEMAN
blueman.com

TIP

Blue Man is for ages three and up. If there's light sensitivity, talk to theater staff ahead of time. They plan separate shows for kids on the autism spectrum; just ask.

GO BEHIND CLOSED DOORS

AT OPEN HOUSE CHICAGO

With 150 sites in approximately 20 neighborhoods and suburbs, Open House Chicago is when sites normally closed to the public throw open their doors to everyone. Held in October—free for attendees—the list of places includes the historic Chicago Board of Trade building, the private Cliff Dwellers Club (a haven for artists, musicians, and the like), backroom spaces at the spectacular Riviera Theater, and tons more. Included for a few years running has been the 11th Floor roof-deck of the Prudential Building, which overlooks Millennium Park and Lake Michigan in the distance; this is a place where you will never stand unless you are a tenant of the building or attend Open House Chicago. This two-day event allows you to check multiple venues off your bucket list—all for free.

Chicago Architecture Center: 312-922-3432
openhousechicago.org

Garden of the Gods,
Shawnee National Forest

SPORTS AND RECREATION

SPELUNK

WHERE RIVER PIRATES ONCE DWELLED

Spelunking (cave exploring) can be done at Cave-in-Rock, located where the southeast tip of Illinois meets the Ohio River. This 55-foot-wide cavern was discovered in 1739 by a French explorer and dubbed Caverne dans Le Roc; the name stuck, though now we say it in English. With an opening in the top of the cave that acts as a natural chimney, this was a perfect hideout for river pirates in the late 1700s, and for other unsavory types in the early 1800s. Lore indicates that the cave housed a brothel, gambling den, and a tavern run by thieves who would lure people in, and then rob and kill them. Eventually, the cave was taken over by people intent on establishing a settlement nearby; they even held church services in the cave. Talk about your 360-degree pivot. Cave-in-Rock is the name of the village, cave, and nearby state park, which offers trails, camping, a lodge, and restaurant. As you enter the cave, look for cliff sparrows whose mud nests cling to the cave's outer walls; usually, they'll peek out to say hello.

1 New State Park Rd., Cave-in-Rock, 618-289-4325
www2.illinois.gov/dnr/parks/pages/caveinrock.aspx

DISCOVER THE THRILL
OF WHITEWATER RAPIDS

For whitewater rafting in Illinois, you can head to one of two places. For a short-run, go to Yorkville, which has an open-use, 1,100-foot-long whitewater course on the Fox River. Built as a bypass chute around the Glen D. Palmer Dam, paddlers can now safely circumvent the dam. A concrete path allows paddlers to walk their apparatus back to the beginning of the chute if they're apt to repeat the fun. To rent a canoe or kayak in Yorkville, call the Yak Shak.

For a long-run, hit Vermillion River Rafting (VRR) in Oglesby, where you'll find a three to four hour, nine-and-a-half mile whitewater experience, including 14 sets of "class 1 and 2" rapids (and some "class 3" rapids if the river is high). This is completely self-guided, and law requires that participants watch safety videos in advance (provided by VRR). The high season for VRR runs from May to mid-July; anything outside of that time is dependent on rain. If in doubt, phone first. And definitely pay close attention to all safety protocols.

Marge Kline Whitewater Course
301 E Hydraulic, Yorkville, 630-479-8074
yorkville.il.us/facilities

Vermillion River Rafting
779 N 2249th St., Oglesby, 815-667-5242
vermillionriverrafting.com

BIKE THE LAKEFRONT TRAIL
ALONG LAKE MICHIGAN

Biking Chicago's lakefront lets you cover lots of ground. The 18-mile paved lakefront trail runs from Ardmore Street (5800 N Sheridan Rd.) to the north, through the heart of Chicago, and then south to 71st Street. You can BYO bike or rent one. Bike and Roll Chicago rents bicycles seasonally from Navy Pier and year-round from Millennium Park. In business for two decades is Bobby's Bike Hike Chicago, which offers traditional and electric bike rentals, and holds themed bike rides. Chicago Bike Adventures is another high-rated bike tour company that also offers bike rentals. Whatever kind of bike you choose, this is one of the best ways to enjoy Chicago's vast lakeshore.

Bike and Roll Chicago
312-729-1000
bikechicago.com

Bobby's Bike Hike Chicago
312-245-9300
bobbysbikehike.com

Chicago Bike Adventures
773-209-1311
chicagobikeadventures.com

TIP

A word about Chicago's bike share system, called Divvy. It's a good system for regular users, but it's not the best option for tourists. Stations near busy attractions often have long wait times, and the cost can be high if you keep the bike too long.

45

RUN THE RIVER TO RIVER RELAY RACE
IN SOUTHERN ILLINOIS

There's something about the camaraderie of a relay race . . . reaching the end of an enormous number of miles . . . together. Runners are lone wolves, but they dream of relay races in exotic places. As it turns out, Southern Illinois has just the spot. In the heart of Shawnee National Forest is an annual 80-mile River to River Relay Race that extends from the Mississippi River valley at the southwest edge of Illinois (southwest of Murphysboro) to the Ohio River (at Golconda). This race winds through hills, breathtaking beauty, and . . . more hills. Held each April, eight-person running teams divvy up 24 sections of the race so that each runner runs three sections. But be forewarned, race registrations fill up fast. They have nine major divisions as well as some special divisions (e.g., Academic, Armed Forces, Happy Families, Old Friends). Race dates are posted to their website years in advance, which means you can plan for two or three years from now to check this item off your bucket list.

River to River Relay Race
rrr.olm.net

JUMP OUT OF AN AIRPLANE

WITH SKYDIVE CHICAGO

Fearless first-time jumpers step right up to the open door of an airborne airplane. But don't worry, jumping "tandem" means you'll be harnessed to a skilled skydiving pro with Skydive Chicago. Tandem skydiving is how it all starts. Only after taking classes, which Skydive Chicago offers, would you be allowed to jump alone.

More than a place for one-time experiences, Skydive Chicago is more of a resort. They have rental cabins, a campground with tent spaces, a pond with a white sand beach, fishing, and volleyball courts. This is where skydivers spend days at a time, jumping days in a row.

If you've always meant to get around to this bucket list item, this is the place to do it.

3215 E 1969th Rd., Ottawa, 815-433-0000
skydivechicago.com

47

HOLD A RUSTIC REUNION
IN A BUNKHOUSE

When trying to gather the family (or your pals) in one place, we play 20 questions. Where shall we go? What's there to do there? What can we afford? Look no more. Kendall County Forest Preserve District's Hoover Forest Preserve offers the best of nature for families or friends who want togetherness—with a dash of separation—and who don't want to break the bank. The answer is . . . book a bunkhouse. A bunkhouse in a forest setting is a bit like camping, but with heat, A/C, running water, and a full-size kitchen. Hoover Preserve has three bunkhouses to choose from, and each sleeps up to 32 people. And yes, they're called bunkhouses because all bedrooms have bunkbeds (I call the bottom bunk!). With the Fox River nearby, plus six miles of trails that meander past creeks and ravines, Hoover Preserve promises plenty of outdoor activities. So, pack your hiking shoes, fishing pole, and plan an unforgettable getaway.

11285 Fox Rd., Yorkville, 630-553-4025
kendallforest.com

DOWNHILL SKI
AT CHESTNUT MOUNTAIN RESORT

Oh yes, Illinois has downhill skiing! But you must head to the northwest tip of the state to find it. Chestnut Mountain Resort touts 220 acres of rolling hills with a 475-foot vertical drop, 19 ski runs, and plenty of lifts. Their lodge enables you to play all day and stay overnight. After a full day of activities, grab a hot toddy, soak in the pool or jacuzzi, or have dinner at their on-site restaurant. If you book one of their slopeside rooms, you'll be able to keep an eye on the action from indoors. Note that guest rooms face either the woods/parking lot or the Mississippi River/slopes. And as the story of room rates goes, staying mid-week saves cool cash.

8700 W Chestnut Mountain Rd., Galena, 800-397-1320
chestnutmtn.com

TIP

The resort is just five miles from downtown Galena, where you'll find shops, historical tours, and culinary options, including Fried Green Tomatoes, a dinner-only, upscale Italian restaurant whose reputation is long and superb.

TEST YOUR SKILLS
AT COG HILL GOLF CLUB'S DUBSDREAD/NO.4

The only golf course in Illinois included in *Golf Digest*'s Top 100 Public Courses is Cog Hill No. 4, nicknamed "Dubsdread." (A dub is a poor golfer.) Designed by architect Dick Wilson, whose work extends to two other continents, the course fulfills the vision held by club owner Joe Jemsek, who wanted a fourth course at Cog that was "as good or better" than the private country clubs across the nation. Architect Dick Wilson designed courses from 1947 through his death in 1965, and Dubsdread was one of his last. Also called "No. 4," this course has tight landing areas as well as Wilson's signature heavily bunkered, large greens. Jemsek got his wish—a public course that has hosted PGA and USGA tournaments over the years. You, too, can golf where the pros golf. Give it your best shot!

12294 Archer Ave., Lemont, 630-257-5872
coghillgolf.com

TOUR HISTORIC
STARVED ROCK STATE PARK

The state's most visited state park sits atop a 125-foot sandstone butte, and is home to exquisite canyons, bluffs, waterfalls, and wildlife. Most of these features are reachable by trekking the park's 13 miles of hiking trails. Set along the Illinois River, the park harbors more than 200 species of birds, including bald eagles that flock to the dam adjacent to the State Park Visitor Center trail. (Another place from which to view the eagles is the Illinois Waterway Visitor Center, 950 N 27 Road/Dee Bennett Road, Ottawa, directly across the river from Starved Rock Visitor Center.)

Booking a guided walking tour is the best orientation to the area, but if you're not big on three-hour hikes, you might consider a narrated trolley tour. Or stop by the Visitor Center for a map, and meander on your own.

Starved Rock also has a historic lodge, and offers guest rooms, cabins, a fine dining restaurant, and a pub. The lodge's back deck looks out over the river, which means, no matter where you're at within the park, you're surrounded by natural beauty.

Visitor Center
2668 E 873 Rd., Oglesby, 815-667-4726
www2.illinois.gov/dnr/parks/pages/starvedrock.aspx

Lodge
1 Lodge Way, Oglesby, 815-667-4211
starvedrocklodge.com

HIKE
AT MIDEWIN TALLGRASS PRAIRIE

What was once Joliet Army Ammunition Plant is now Midewin Tallgrass Prairie, with hiking trails, one of which meanders near some bison, and another that leads to old bomb shelters that housed TNT during WWII. Camouflaged by dirt, grass, and shrubs, the shelters can be reached via a two-mile hike. When this old army base underwent restoration to a prairie, most of the 400 bomb shelters were razed, but a handful were saved so that people could learn the arsenal history of the land. Just follow Henslow Trail south from Midewin Iron Bridge Trailhead; the trail goes over State Rt. 53, and then veers south to a paved road. Here, you'll see a sign pointing toward Explosives Road Trailway—follow the sign and you'll end up at the bunkers. As you approach them from behind, they'll look like hills. To stand at the base of a bunker is surreal. Who were the soldiers that worked here? And what happened to the explosives stored here?

Midewin's small herd of bison grazes in an area southeast of Iron Bridge Trailhead. They're hard to find, but you might get lucky, especially if you have binoculars.

Midewin Iron Bridge Trailhead
State Rt. 53, Elwood

Midewin Tallgrass Prairie Welcome Center
30239 State Rt. 53, Wilmington, 815-423-6370

ATTEND A FIGHTING ILLINI FOOTBALL GAME

Each fall, energized fans descend on Memorial Stadium, home of the Fighting Illini, the football team of the University of Illinois-Urbana/Champaign (UIUC). Adjacent to the stadium is Grange Grove, where tailgating is an art form. There's live music and a family fun zone—all to get fans jazzed and ready for the big game. Grange Grove is a first come/first served venue that allows fans to set up chairs, tables, or small tents the night before, or as early as 7 a.m. on game day. A couple hours before kick-off, the whole team walks through Grange Grove on their way into the stadium. Talk about your cheering fans. When the stands finally fill up, the game kicks off and the stadium goes wild. This is a big-ticket experience without the big-ticket prices.

1402 S 1st St., Champaign, 217-333-3631
fightingillini.com

53

WALK IN
THE GARDEN OF THE GODS

How can you not be drawn to a place with a name like this? Garden of the Gods Recreation Area is on the eastern edge of Shawnee National Forest—a forest that takes up a good chunk of the southernmost section of the state and consists of 289,000 acres of natural wonders. At Garden of the Gods, there are rock formations and cliffs that have been formed over millions of years, the result of an ancient sea that covered the area, and then retreated southward. Among sandstone behemoths is a wilderness trail system that winds 16 miles. The shortest and most accessible trail is the quarter-mile Observation Trail, which has moderate slopes and some stairs. Though easier than most, this trail is still in an area of high cliffs, poison ivy, and venomous snakes. To be forewarned is to be ready. "Learn before you go," is the best advice when venturing into nature—anywhere in the world. The wilderness trails vary in difficulty and length, and the Forest Service offers the best maps/information.

Garden of the Gods Rd., just north of Karbers Ridge Rd., Herod, 618-658-2111
fs.usda.gov/recarea/shawnee

SEE
LITTLE GRAND CANYON

A grand canyon in Illinois? Yes! This geologic marvel is on the western edge of Shawnee National Forest, just six miles from the Mississippi River. Carved by water, this deep box canyon requires a moderately difficult hike to bluffs that overlook it. For full exposure, take the three-mile loop hike in and out of the canyon. Bring your endurance (and water) and wear your climbing shoes, because the descent to the canyon floor is considered difficult by trail standards. For those less inclined to do the full loop, use the Canyon Overlook trail, which is just under a half-mile from the parking lot (0.8 mile round trip). This National Natural Landmark is a true bucket list destination.

Five miles west of State Rt. 127 at Etherton Rd., Pomona Township
618-833-8576, fs.usda.gov/shawnee

ATTEND A
CHICAGO SKY WNBA GAME

Chi Town is also Sky Town, home of the WNBA team, the Chicago Sky. A team of skilled professionals with All-Star power, the Sky won their first WNBA championship in 2021. WNBA history doesn't go back as far as men's leagues. It was 1972 when Title IX was passed, which granted females the right to participate in organized school sports. With that, the groundwork was laid for women's sports on the national stage. The WNBA was formed in 1996, and the first games were held in fall 1997. Today, the Chicago Sky offers some of the best moments in professional basketball, and they play at Wintrust Arena, a part of McCormick Place Square. You'll find that McCormick's Parking Lot A is most convenient (set your GPS to 2301 S Prairie Avenue). As for Wintrust Arena, bring nothing but your sportsmanship and a plastic bag for any belongings that won't fit in your pocket (no purses or bags allowed). Let's support women's sports!

Wintrust Arena
200 E Cermak Rd., Chicago

Chicago Sky
312-791-6900
sky.wnba.com

56

ROAM "THE STREETS"
AT GIANT CITY STATE PARK

Four thousand acres make up Giant City State Park, which derives its name from its massive sandstone formations. Passageways between these formations are dubbed Giant City Streets, and you can traverse them via the Giant City Nature Trail. "Breathtaking" is the best word to describe this GIANT experience. With an overwhelming array of beauty and history (including a Native American stone wall erected more than a thousand years ago), the best place to start is at the Visitor Center, where a ranger can give pointers on how to find the things you hope to see. Be sure to check out the State Park Lodge, built in the 1930s of white oak timber; it includes a restaurant and gift shop. On the far side of the lodge's parking lot is a water tower with steps leading to a 50-foot observation deck that affords a view above the treetops. The panoramic view is worth the climb. Located just 10 miles southeast of Carbondale, this state park has an otherworldly element to it.

235 Giant City Rd., Makanda, 618-457-4836
www2.illinois.gov/dnr/parks/pages/giantcity.aspx

CHEER FOR THE CUBS
AT THE HISTORIC WRIGLEY FIELD

Wrigley Field should be on every bucket list of baseball fields to see. Not just because it's the second-oldest major league field in the nation, which it is. And not just because it's been home to the Cubbies (as Chicagoans call them) since 1916, the only National League charter team that is still playing in its original city. And not just because of its super-charged fan base and its super cool location in a north neighborhood of Chicago, surrounded by hip hangouts. Wrigley Field is a bucket list ballfield because of all these things, plus because of its highly recognizable ivy-covered, brick outfield wall with bleachers perched atop. Having so many residential neighbors meant the Chicago Cubs franchise went 72 years without night games; they were the last major league field to (be allowed to) add lights. If you're in the mood for a pre-game or post-game beverage at a local bar, the Cubby Bear, across from Wrigley Field, is an institution. Or give Harry Caray's a try, just a block from the field.

1060 W Addison St., Chicago, 773-388-8270
mlb.com/cubs

The Berlin Wall

(1961–1989)

"Mr. Gorbachev, tear down this wall."
Ronald W. Reagan, June 12, 1987

Berlin Wall, Eureka

World's Largest Mailbox, Casey

Egyptian Theatre, DeKalb

Superman's Hometown, Metropolis

Grosse Pointe Lighthouse, Evanston

Lovejoy Homestead UGRR Station, Princeton

Woodstock Opera House

White squirrel, Olney

CONFEDERATE
CEMETERY

"LET US CROSS THE RIVER
AND REST IN THE SHADE
OF THE TREES"
GENERAL T. JACKSON, USA

ROCK ISLAND ARSENAL

Confederate Cemetery, Rock Island

Illinois Statehouse, Vandalia

Caboose Lodging in Wildlife Prairie Park, Hanna City

Giant City State Park, Makanda

Graue Mill, UGRR Station, Oak Brook

Lincoln Heritage Museum, Lincoln

Treehouse Glamping at Timber Ridge, Elizabethtown

Great Galena Balloon Race, Galena.
Courtesy of Shannon Jones

Carl Sandburg Statue, Galesburg

Illinois State Fair and Route 66 Experience, Springfield

GLAMP
IN A TREEHOUSE

No, I'm not kidding. Yes, you'll have to climb into a tree to sleep. But there are stairs (no ladder required). With floorboards and walls held up by tree branches, this is one of those places you must see to believe. Timber Ridge has hosted guests in their treetops for years. Located in the Shawnee National Forest, and a stone's throw from the Garden of the Gods, this means your stay will be populated with beauty, fresh air, and plenty of wildlife. Timber Ridge has two treehouses, plus a few cabins, all in a connected area. This means you can phone a friend! That is, invite friends or family to come along, too. Or just go and then make your friends jealous with your amazing adventure stories.

546 N Iron Furnace Rd., Elizabethtown, 618-264-9091
timberridgeoutpost.com

TIP

Timber Ridge is amid the wilderness, so plan to pack in all your supplies or you'll need to drive back out again, via winding, hilly country roads. It's 10 miles to Elizabethtown proper.

59

WATCH THE SKY
DURING THE GREAT GALENA BALLOON RACE

There are many reasons to visit Galena—President Grant's homestead, the state's "driftless zone," and a vibrant historic downtown district. But the biggest draw might be the Great Galena Balloon Race that's been held for more than 20 years, drawing balloonists from across America. To see one airborne balloon is quite cool, but to see 10 or 15 or more is magical. Held in June at Eagle Ridge Resort, spectators pay a small fee, with proceeds going to the Juvenile Diabetes Foundation. What sets Galena's race apart from other balloon festivals is its history. The same person who founded this race is still there, year after year. Galena On the Fly, housed at Eagle Ridge, runs rides for the race, as well as apart from the race, from May through October. It's important to recognize that high winds can suspend airborne activities. For anyone bringing kids, the Great Race grounds include inflatables and other fun stuff—plus it's for charity. So, bring your patience, good cheer, and a lawn chair, and see something so unique, you'll remember it forever.

400 Eagle Ridge Dr., Galena, 815-777-5000
greatgalenaballoonrace.com

Galena On the Fly
815-777-2747

ROCK CLIMB
AT HOLY BOULDERS

Rock climbers speak a different language. There's bouldering and belaying, and climbers are always looking for new "problems" (climbing term) in nature. Lo and behold, Southern Illinois offers some of the best rock-climbing terrain in the Midwest. When climbers discovered Holy Boulders, situated on the west edge of Shawnee National Forest, they approached the farmer who owned it, who gave them permission to climb there. When the land went up for sale, the Illinois Climbers Association (ICA) bought it. To help pay off the mortgage, and fuel upkeep, ICA hosts the Pilgrimage at Holy Boulders every November. This is when spectators are allowed into the area. If you've never witnessed rock climbing in nature (common in Colorado), you're missing out. It's simply amazing.

1 Tripps Ln., Pomona, 612-730-3907
ilclimbers.org

TIP

Shawnee Trails Wilderness Outfitters has been selling gear for climbing (and backpacking and much more) since 1979; they've built a reputation on hard-to-find equipment.

222 W Freeman St., Carbondale, 618-529-2313

Black Hawk Historic Site, Rock Island

CULTURE AND HISTORY

SPOT ABE LINCOLN
IN THE CITY OF LINCOLN

See the only city in the world named for Abe Lincoln before he became president—Lincoln, Illinois. Here is where you can see a huge Honest Abe at the helm of the world's largest covered wagon (per Guinness). Plus, Lincoln is the seat of Logan County, with a courthouse built on the footprint of the one where Mr. Lincoln practiced law immediately preceding his presidency. Courthouse Square, listed on the National Register of Historic Places, has Civil War markers that show how proud Lincolnites must have been to fight for the Union. For something quirky, stand at the east corner of Courthouse Square and look east across the intersection at the roof of City Hall—it's a phone booth . . . on the roof. Why? Ask a Lincolnite!

On your list of "seeing Lincoln in Lincoln" is the Historic Train Depot, the site of the town's christening by Mr. Lincoln himself (find the watermelon sculpture). Also, visit the Lincoln Heritage Museum where they house rare artifacts of Lincoln's life—including a lock of his hair.

destinationlogancountyil.com

ALL IN LINCOLN

Largest Covered Wagon
1750 5th St.

Logan County Courthouse
601 Broadway St.

Historic Depot/Visitor Center
101 N Chicago St.

Lincoln Heritage Museum
300 Keokuk St.

SPEND TIME
AT DUSABLE BLACK HISTORY MUSEUM

DuSable Black History Museum is America's oldest independent African American museum; an affiliate of the world-renowned Smithsonian Institution; and has amassed 15,000 pieces of historical memorabilia, including paintings, print works, sculptures, and more. It is fitting that DuSable Black History Museum is named for the Haitian-born Black man, Jean Baptist Point du Sable, who established the prosperous trading settlement that became Chicago. At DuSable, you'll find performances, lectures, exhibits, and archives, all in a place where history has never been forgotten nor revised. Here, there are firsthand accounts and curated collections that teach about slavery, emancipation, the Red Summer of 1919, plus the accomplishments of groups and individuals such as the 369th regiment of WWI, W. E. B. DuBois, Dr. King, and countless others. Sharing the past is DuSable's way of connecting what was with what is—a path forward for all.

740 E 56th Pl., Chicago, 773-947-0600
dusablemuseum.org

TOUCH A PIECE
OF THE BERLIN WALL

President Ronald Reagan famously said, "Mr. Gorbachev, tear down this wall." The year was 1987 and Reagan stood on the West Germany side of the Berlin Wall. Reagan was an Illinois boy and credits his attendance at Eureka College for setting him on a path of success. It's at Eureka College that you'll find the Ronald Reagan Museum and a narrative of his life, as told through childhood photos and other memorabilia. When you enter the museum, you might find a jar of individually wrapped jelly beans (but of course!). Just outside the museum's doors is the Reagan Peace Garden with a chunk of the Berlin Wall, and 22 pieces of rebar poking out from its top. When you touch it, you're touching history.

300 E College Ave., Eureka, 888-438-7352
eureka.edu

TIP

Park in Burgess West parking lot, which is behind Burgess Memorial Hall (corner of College Avenue and Burgess Street). A map posted at this parking lot shows the entire campus.

SOAK UP THE CITY NAMED FOR JOHN QUINCY ADAMS

In Adams County is the city of Quincy, named for the sixth US president, whose election coincided with the naming of this Illinois county and its county seat in 1825. Located along the Mississippi River, Quincy is a river town with views, both natural and manmade (architecture), that are downright spectacular. One of the first sites to visit is Quinsippi Island, reachable by traversing a one-lane bridge. On it is Log Cabin Village, and if you follow Quinsippi Road to the southern tip of the island, you can view Bayview Bridge, the cable-stayed bridge that connects Quincy to Missouri.

Downtown Quincy is where you'll see almost unparalleled architectural beauty, beginning with the tourist center inside Villa Kathrine, a cream-colored castle built atop a bluff on the Mississippi.

Another MUST is Indian Mounds Park—a drive-through park with storyboards that's both archeologically important and sacred. Its entrance is on RJ Peters Dr., just west of the intersection of 8th St. and RJ Peters Dr. A public pool is part of this complex; just go past it and absorb the history.

Quincy Visitors Bureau/Villa Kathrine
532 Gardner Expy., Quincy, 800-978-4748
seequincy.com

65

VISIT ILLINOIS'S
SECOND STATE CAPITAL IN VANDALIA

When Illinois became a state in 1818, Kaskaskia was the capital because of its location on the Mississippi River. But the river changed course, and so did the state. By 1819, the state capital moved to Vandalia, and it was here that Abe Lincoln began his political career as a state representative. Two previous Vandalia statehouses are no more. The third, built in 1836, still stands and it's the oldest statehouse in Illinois. Lifting the latch on the huge front door to walk inside is like stepping back in time—to Mr. Lincoln's time.

Vandalia also has the Fayette County Museum, where you'll see a splitting froe with the initials "A. L." scratched into it, owned by the "Railsplitter" himself. The story behind it is fascinating.

315 W Gallatin St., Vandalia, 618-283-1161
www2.illinois.gov/dnrhistoric/experience/sites/southwest

SEE FABYAN'S
JAPANESE GARDEN AND WINDMILL

George and Nella Fabyan fell in love with the Japanese Pavilion at the 1893 World's Fair, after which, they built their own Japanese garden. Situated amid shade trees, paths meander through the garden, water trickles, and a small bridge arches over a stream, creating an island illusion. Designed for solitude, Fabyan's garden is at the bottom of the hill, away from the villa, and along the Fox River. The river actually sliced through the Fabyan estate, with the rest of their land on the east side. Today, pedestrian bridges connect the two sides. On the east side is now Fabyan Forest Preserve-East, which holds another piece of Fabyan history—a five-story, fully restored windmill. According to experts, it's the best example of an authentic Dutch windmill in the United States.

Fabyan also built a lighthouse on his estate, not far from his garden, for reasons that come with their own funny history.

With the Fox River Trail running along the east bank, what was once one man's land now welcomes the public to walk, bike, and linger.

Fabyan Garden and Villa
1925 S Batavia Ave. Geneva
ppfv.org

Fabyan Windmill
1500 Crissey Ave., Geneva, 630-232-5980
kaneforest.com/fabyan-windmill

TOUR ILLINOIS'S
TWO NATIONAL LANDMARK CAPITOL BUILDINGS IN SPRINGFIELD

Abe Lincoln lived in several Midwest towns, but it was in Springfield that he bought the only home he ever owned. And it was here that, as a lawyer, he tried hundreds of cases before the Illinois Supreme Court, in the structure now called the Old State Capitol—in which he also delivered his House Divided Speech. When he departed Springfield for Washington, the Civil War had just begun.

Springfield also has Illinois's sixth—and current—state capitol building (opened in 1877), with a dome that reaches 361 feet, making it 74 feet taller than the US Capitol. If you've never toured Springfield's two capitol buildings, you must. The artwork alone will make your jaw drop.

Capitol Complex Visitors Center
425 S College St., Springfield, 217-524-6620

To arrange tours, contact the Springfield Convention & Visitor Bureau
800-545-7300

TIP

Twenty miles northwest of Springfield is Lincoln's New Salem State Historic Site, where Honest Abe lived and worked during early adulthood. This reconstructed pioneer village is open year-round.

15588 History Ln., Petersburg, 217-632-4000
lincolnsnewsalem.com

ISLAND HOP
ON ARSENAL ISLAND

The Mississippi River has islands that can be reached by bridge, and Arsenal Island, from which the city of Rock Island derives its name, is the biggest. During the Revolutionary War, Fort Armstrong was on the island, and during the Civil War, the island housed a Confederate Prison. Today, it's home to the Mississippi River Visitor Center (with Locks and Dam 15), plus a museum, national cemetery, Confederate cemetery, and US Army facility. Because of the army's presence, visitors must use the Moline gate and stop to obtain a pass (those with a Military ID Card can enter either gate—Moline or Rock Island). The Mississippi River Visitor Center's outer decks offer a birds-eye view of river traffic in the locks, as well as migrating birds, including white pelicans.

23 Prospect Dr., Moline, 309-782-1337
home.army.mil/ria

TIP

The Mississippi River Visitor Center is a great spot for watching "Floatzilla," an annual event, held in August, hosted by River Action, drawing about 3,000 paddlers from 16 states.

ATTEND
THE AMERICAN INDIAN CENTER'S ANNUAL POWWOW

The American Indian Center of Chicago's (AIC) powwows have been held for seven decades and continue annually each October. This is when native tribal members share culture through dance, drum, song, art, and storytelling. And non-native persons are invited! In fact, a powwow is one of the best ways to learn, as well as enjoy native food. Throughout the two-day event, there are "intertribal dances," where tribes come together and audience members are invited to dance, too. Held in recent years at Schiller Woods in Schiller Park, food trucks sell bison chili and fry bread, Indian Tacos, and other delectables. If you've never seen a little girl wearing a "jingle dress" as she dances, prepare your heart to melt. Attending a powwow is an honor. And a cultural "must."

3401 W Ainslie St., Chicago, 773-275-5871
aicchicago.org

TIP

The AIC offers programs on cooking, crafts, drum, and dance, and they provide gallery space for Native American artists/performers. All are invited into the AIC. Open Monday through Friday, it's best to phone first.

WORK ON AN 1890S-ERA FARM

AT KLINE CREEK FARM

Do more than daydream about what life was like on a farm at the turn of the 20th century. At Kline Creek Farm, guests may perform a variety of farm chores from days of yore, including milking a cow, shearing a sheep, tapping a tree for maple, or helping harvest corn in autumn. Through programming, visitors can learn how to make candy on a wood-burning stove. And if you've never seen a newly born lamb, come in spring. If you want to learn about harvesting ice, which our ancestors had to do in order to keep food cold, come in winter. From farmhouse tours to blacksmithing, and plenty of animals, this place is where history lives (and works).

1N600 County Farm Rd., West Chicago, 630-876-5900
dupageforest.org/kline-creek-farm

TIP

Another 18th-century farm is Volkening Farm in Schaumburg (once a rural German town) with barnyard animals, furnished farmhouse, and guides dressed in period clothing. Volkening's grounds (with trails and arboretum) stay open year-round. The museum and farmhouse are open April to November.

parkfun.com/spring-valley/heritage-farm

EXPERIENCE GEORGE PULLMAN'S
PLANNED INDUSTRIAL TOWN

George Pullman's social experiment was a town populated by employees of his Pullman Palace Car Co., which produced luxury railroad sleeping cars. The town of Pullman—with its industrial plant as the anchor—was the first of its kind in the nation. It had homes where workers lived, stores where they shopped, schools for their kids, plus a bank, theater, library, and even a grand hotel. Built southeast of Chicago in the 1880s, Pullman's planned city remained its own town until 1907 when Chicago annexed it.

Now a National Monument, Pullman is a neighborhood whose residents live in homes built by George Pullman. Market Hall, which once housed stalls brimming with fresh meat and vegetables, upon which factory workers depended, still stands as testament to the organization of the town. Touring the Visitors Center in the old Pullman Company administration/clock tower building is where one begins to absorb the sheer magnitude of what Mr. Pullman built and the ramifications for organized labor. The town of Pullman helped form America's labor movement, and it spurred declaration of Labor Day as a workers' holiday.

National Monument Visitors Center
11001 S Cottage Grove Ave., Chicago, 773-468-9310
nps.gov/pull

72

SEE THE TOWN
THAT JOSEPH SMITH BUILT

A true living museum, Nauvoo brims with the history of the Mormons who gave it its name (Nauvoo is Hebrew for "beautiful place"). After being expelled from Missouri, led by church founder Joseph Smith, early Mormons found a safe haven here, along the east bank of the Mississippi River. And more than 180 years later, the streets, hills, and homes reflect the history of a group seeking religious freedom during America's early decades. The Visitors Center, operated by the Church of Latter Day Saints, provides guided walking tours, as well as carriage, wagon, and ox rides—all of which they offer free as a way of sharing the story of this area.

Nauvoo's location on the Mississippi offers stunning river views. And since Nauvoo Temple draws a large number of church members to the area, lodging is some of the most plentiful and diverse—and reasonable, especially for large groups. Note that Nauvoo is also the location of Illinois's oldest winery, Baxter's, the site of an annual grape festival. Beautiful area with great lodging and great wine? Mais oui!

Nauvoo Visitor Center
290 N Main, Nauvoo, 217-557-2610
nauvoohistoricsites.org/visitor

For lodging, check beautifulnauvoo.com

TAKE A HISTORY OR HAUNTS TOUR
IN ALTON

Alton is known as home to Elijah Lovejoy, murdered in 1837 by an anti-abolitionist mob; thus Lovejoy is called the first martyr of a free press society. In 1857, Abraham Lincoln called Lovejoy's murder "the most important single event that has happened in the new world." For its importance to Black history and the Underground Railroad, Alton is a true destination. It also happens to be one of America's most haunted small towns. So, whether it's history or hauntings that pique your interest, there's a tour for you. Two companies offer year-round tours—Alton Odyssey Tours and Alton Hauntings Tours. (During Halloween, extra tours are added.) In addition, Alton Visitors Center schedules seasonally Underground Railroad tours with renowned historian J. Eric Robinson. Other historically focused tours will bring you to Elijah Lovejoy's memorial, erected decades after his death (after the Civil War when his heroism was recognized).

Altonians are quick to point out that Alton is at the confluence of two rivers, as well as the last place Route 66 touches Illinois at its west edge. And if that weren't enough, one of the most beautiful stretches of the Great River Road runs through this river town.

Alton Odyssey Tours
618-433-1392
altonodysseytours.com

Alton Hauntings Tours
217-791-7859
altonhauntings.com

Visitors Center/Great Rivers and Routes of Southwest Illinois
200 Piasa St., Alton, 800-258-6645
riversandroutes.com

Amtrak Station
1 Golf Rd., Alton

74

EXPLORE
THE NATIONAL MUSEUM OF MEXICAN ART

One of the nation's largest Mexican art collections resides at the National Museum of Mexican Art (NMMA), which makes its home in the Pilsen neighborhood of Chicago. From paintings and textiles to theater and dance, the NMMA offers much to its patrons. Though small, this museum is mighty, and the history of how it came to be is inspiring. It's a story of new immigrants needing assistance, and impoverished neighborhoods displaced by an expressway and a university, and finally, the banding together of these sidelined citizens to create their own space in Pilsen. If you don't know the history of the 1848 treaty that ended the US–Mexican War, reading up on it will foster a greater appreciation for this fountain of culture. Admission is free.

1852 W 19th St., Chicago, 312-738-1503
nationalmuseumofmexicanart.org

TIP

NMMA and Pilsen pull out the stops for the traditional Mexican holiday of Día de Muertos (Oct. 31–Nov. 2) with special family-friendly activities, plus the museum offers late hours.

LEARN ABOUT
PREHISTORIC MISSISSIPPIAN MOUNDS (STATEWIDE)

Of 11 cultural World Heritage Sites in the United States, one is a vast collection of mounds (Cahokia). Most mounds are burial sites of VIPs (chiefs or leaders), but the biggest mounds held ceremonial buildings and homes of the elite. Following is a list of some of these sacred sites—places where we can learn about the people who dwelled on the prairies before Europeans sought resources here. There are examples of science, engineering, and highly structured communities. These destinations, at least one of which must be on your bucket list, are great learning opportunities for children.

Cahokia Mounds in Collinsville dates back to 700 AD and is a World Heritage Site and State Historic Site. Here, "Monks Mound" is the largest prehistoric earthen construction in all of the Americas, covering 14 acres at its base and rising 100 feet. Though specific tribal history is unknown, it's named for the Cahokia tribe of the Illiniwek (Illinois) confederacy. A striking element at Cahokia is Woodhenge, with its five circular sun calendars with large, evenly spaced, red cedar posts. If you arrive at Woodhenge at sunrise on one of the equinoxes or solstices, look for the post that aligns with the rising sun. Located near St. Louis, Cahokia's museum underwent structural renovation in 2022, during which the museum was closed; re-opening is set for 2023.

Dickson Mounds State Museum in Lewistown sits where there was once a large Mississippian village. Previously owned by the Dickson family, one of the Dickson sons began excavating mounds on their farm and later sold it to the state in 1945. Today, Dickson Mounds Museum is one of the few large on-site archaeological museums in North America. The museum has a campus of 235 acres that includes walking trails. Though it feels like the museum is in the middle of nowhere, its location in the Spoon River Valley means that you must read Edgar Lee Masters's *Spoon River Anthology* before you visit (the audio version is a real treat), and then stop at Oak Hill Cemetery in Lewistown, where a map points out the graves "on the hill."

Indian Mounds Park in Quincy is basically a driving tour, with a road that winds its way past several mounds. Signs proclaim its archaeological importance (no digging!) and offer lessons on geology and the history of the people who dwelled here. Part of the Quincy Park District, the best directions are: enter off RJ Peters Drive about 100 feet west of its intersection with S 8th Street. This one-way park road runs past mounds, and then past the city swimming pool, and continues on to more mounds. You'll want to see it all.

Two other sites include **Albany Mounds** and **Kincaid Mounds**, both State Historic Sites. Albany Mounds is in the Mississippi River town of Albany, north of Moline, and has 39 burial mounds interspersed among a rural, prairie grass setting. Kincaid Mounds, near the Ohio River, southeast of Unionville, has a number of mounds that encircle what used to be a plaza (flat space used for public gatherings). Interpretive signs at both Albany and Kincaid Mounds speak of organized village life as it existed for the Mississippian culture tribes. Though no comparison to Cahokia or Dickson, these sites are still sacred and worth a visit.

As an example of mounds that can be found here and there around Illinois (almost always near rivers), **Briscoe Mounds Historic Site** in Channahon contains just two mounds. Named for the family who owned a farm where the mounds were found, it's perched along the Des Plaines River, with a tiny lot that fits maybe two cars. For GPS, use 25000 W Front St., or go about 1,000 feet east of the intersection of Front and Fryer Streets.

DISCOVER STATIONS
ON THE UNDERGROUND RAILROAD

During America's horrific slave era, Illinois was a free state surrounded by slave states to the west (Missouri) and south (Kentucky and beyond). Thus, a steady stream of Freedom Seekers sought assistance in Illinois along what is called the Underground Railroad (UGRR)—a series of organized safe places. From America's first Black town in Brooklyn (near St. Louis) to various points around the state, Illinois became known as a place of refuge. In the spirit of those who harbored Freedom Seekers journeying toward Canada, following are a few sights you should see.

Woodlawn Farm, just east of Jacksonville, is at the end of a dusty country road. Michael and Jane Huffaker founded this 160-acre farm in 1824, after which, Michael built four small cabins for farmhands, who were free Black families. This farm's four cabins served as a means to hide Freedom Seekers in plain sight because it was widely known that Huffaker's Black farmhands were free. Today, the farm is a living museum, operated by the Morgan County Historical Society, and is open seasonally.

1463 Gierke Ln., Jacksonville, 309-678-7716
woodlawnfarm.com

In Oak Brook (Chicago west suburb) is **Graue Mill**, which was a regular stop on the UGRR. Founded in 1852 by Frederick Graue, this waterwheel gristmill ground wheat and corn, and also housed Freedom Seekers in its cellar. Today, Graue Mill and Museum is open Thursday through Sunday from April to November, with a full program schedule and permanent UGRR exhibit.

3800 York Rd., Oak Brook, 630-655-2090
grauemill.org

Owen Lovejoy's home in Princeton was one of the most important stations on the UGRR in Illinois because he openly proclaimed his willingness to assist Freedom Seekers. When Owen's brother, Elijah, was murdered in Alton after publishing anti-slavery views in his paper, Owen Lovejoy became an outspoken and ardent abolitionist. Today, the homestead is open from May to September or by appointment. Touring this home illustrates the heroism that was a Lovejoy family tradition.

Rt. 3/Peru St., Princeton, 815-879-9151
nps.gov

77

RIDE
A MULE-POWERED CANAL BOAT

When the Illinois & Michigan (I&M) Canal opened in 1848, it connected the Great Lakes to the Illinois River, and created a water highway from the East Coast to the Mighty Mississippi and beyond to the Gulf of Mexico. This essentially put northern Illinois and Chicago at the crossroads of middle America. The canal's contribution to Chicago's rapid growth cannot be overstated. What's surprising is that, with the canal's maximum depth of 6 feet and width of 60 feet, it couldn't accommodate huge boats; thus, mules pulled the boats. (Mules are sturdier than horses and live longer.)

You, too, can travel by a mule-powered canal boat, coordinated by the I&M Canal Visitor Center. Your tour guide, dressed in period clothing, begins with a Mule Tending 101 talk, and then it's time to board the boat and drift back in time.

I&M Visitor Center
754 1st St., LaSalle, 815-223-1851
iandmcanal.org

TIP

The path that the mule uses is also the I&M bike path, and the I&M Canal Corridor Association provides a rental station at the I&M Visitor Center. Float, pedal, go!

TOUR ILLINOIS'S
LARGEST ROUND BARN

Seeing a round barn is like seeing a bald eagle in the wild—both surprising and thrilling. Though round and polygonal barns are sprinkled around the country, they are more prevalent in the Midwest. And Ryan's Round Barn is the state's largest and a true architectural wonder. Since 1984, a group of volunteers (originally a large group, down to two in late 2022) has worked to preserve the barn, and they've welcomed and educated tens of thousands about the technology of circular barns. The magic is in the use of space. With pie-shaped pens, cattle gather around a circular feed trough that encircles the center silo. Ryan's Round Barn also has a unique feature—underground tanks below the sloped ground floor collected liquid waste, later used as fertilizer. If you like barns, you're going to love this one.

The barn is inside the Johnson-Sauk Trail State Recreational Area
28616 Sauk Trail Rd., Kewanee, 309-721-0305
facebook.com/ryansroundbarn

TIP

This barn's location within a state recreational area comes with options for hiking, camping, and boating. The campground also has one "primitive cabin," with a full-size bed, bunk beds, and HVAC system (but no running water). Call the park at 309-853-2425.

VISIT
GROSSE POINT LIGHTHOUSE

With 60 miles of Lake Michigan coastline and major shipping lanes entering and leaving the port of Chicago in the mid-1800s, Illinois has seen a multitude of shipwrecks. But it was Lake Michigan's version of the *Titanic* that finally led to relocation of the Chicago port lighthouse from "Chicago Pier" to Grosse Point in Evanston. It was September 1860, the passenger steamer's name was the *Lady Elgin*, and in the wee hours of the night, in a storm, she was hit by another boat and sunk. Almost 300 people drowned. Grosse Point Lighthouse opened in 1873, only after the city of Evanston petitioned the US government to build a lighthouse there. The rest of the history is at the lighthouse interpretive center, which is open seasonally, though the grounds are open year-round. The grounds consist of the original lighthouse keeper's home, two fog horn houses out back, plus gardens with interpretive signage. There are even steps that lead to a small beach.

2601 N Sheridan Dr., Evanston, 847-328-6961
grossepointlighthouse.net

MEET THE FIRST AMERICAN WOMAN
TO EARN THE NOBEL PEACE PRIZE

Jane Addams was a social reformer and advocate for women, children, and immigrants. But before she achieved international fame, she was born and raised in Cedarville, just 45 miles west of Rockford. Interstate 90, which passes mere miles from Cedarville, is named in her honor—"Jane Addams Tollway." Born in 1860 at 415 N Mill Street, the home still stands but is privately owned. Farther north on Mill Street is Cedarville Cemetery, where the great lady rests.

Addams's biggest impact was through Jane Addams Hull-House Settlement, which provided educational opportunities for immigrants, childcare for working (impoverished) mothers, an employment bureau, and library. The settlement eventually grew to 13 buildings. What remains today is the museum, which includes Hull Home (a National Landmark) and the Residents Dining Hall.

Jane Addams Hull-House Museum
800 S Halsted, Chicago, 312-413-5353
hullhousemuseum.org

TIP

Cedarville Historical Society, open seasonally, offers Addams family information at their museum.

450 W 2nd St., Cedarville, phone first, 815-990-0417

81

STAND ON
THE ROCKFORD PEACHES' BASEBALL FIELD

When people hear of the All-American Girls Professional Baseball League (AAGPBL), they think of the 1992 movie, *A League of Their Own*. That movie highlighted the AAGPBL's most successful team—the Rockford Peaches—who played at Beyer Stadium from 1943 to 1954. After falling into disrepair (and most of the stadium being razed), it's been renovated. Back are the ball diamond, scoreboard, dugouts, and fencing. Beyer Stadium is now a park where visitors can enter through the original gate house, descend limestone stairs, and walk onto the field. A walk of fame bears signs that explain the history of the AAGPBL (founded by P. Wrigley, Chicago Cubs owner), and there are photos of Peaches players who called this stadium home.

A pilgrimage here is a must for women's sports history fans. At this writing, plans have been approved for a future International Women's Baseball Museum to be built at the north end of Beyer Stadium. For now, there's no dedicated parking for Beyer Stadium, nor street parking, so it's best to visit on a weekend, when Beyer Early Childhood Center/School's parking lot is empty (next-door on 15th Avenue).

245 15th Ave., Rockford
gorockfordpeaches.com/peaches-fan-trail

TOUR
FRANK LLOYD WRIGHT'S HOME AND STUDIO

Wright's home and studio is a mecca for architectural aficionados. This is where, in 1898, he built an addition to his home and formed a studio that pioneered his unique vision. Famous for merging the indoor with the outdoor through use of natural light, fully one-third of his life's work was produced within the walls of his Oak Park studio. Today, you can tour his home/studio and walk in his footsteps. What elements does a studio need in order to further the creativity of someone like Wright? This place holds the answers. The neighborhood around Wright's home brims with his architecture too. In fact, Oak Park contains the largest collection of buildings designed by Wright, including Unity Temple, one of eight structures that comprise Wright's architecture as a United States World Heritage Site.

951 Chicago Ave., Oak Park, 312-994-4000
flwright.org

TIP

Other Wright masterpieces dot the Chicago area, including The Rookery building and Frederick C. Robie House. Farther downstate is the B. Harley Bradley House in Kankakee (wright1900.org) and the Dana-Thomas House in Springfield (www2.illinois.gov/dnrhistoric); both offer tours.

VISIT GALESBURG,
BIRTHPLACE OF CARL SANDBURG

Carl Sandburg's anthology, *Chicago Poems*, is iconic, with his poem, "Chicago," where he coined, "City of Big Shoulders." The Carl Sandburg State Historic Site is one of those places you might think requires a brief stop, but two hours later, you're in the backyard, following the Quotation Walk (his phrases etched into stones) to Remembrance Rock, which sits atop the ashes of Carl and his wife Lillian. The museum complex is actually two homes, one used for the museum, and the tiny three-room home next door is where Sandburg was born in 1878.

While in Galesburg, you must also visit the three-block historic Seminary Street commerce district. Along this section of Seminary, you'll find some sweet shops, including Mother Goosebumps (toys), Cornucopia (natural food market), plus a creperie, fine chocolates, ice cream shop (with allergen-free fare), plus a store filled with the work of local artists (ask about the soldered pieces by one of their oldest artists). And if you're so inclined, there's a train museum at the sound end of the Seminary shopping district.

Carl Sandburg State Historic Site
313 E 3rd St., Galesburg, 309-342-2361
sandburg.org

Seminary Street District
seminarystreet.com

84

LEARN 1800S-ERA PRISON LIFE

AT OLD JOLIET PRISON

If you found yourself in prison in the 1800s, no matter the crime, life was hell. Joliet Prison, built in 1858, is a testament to this fact. Until a warden intent on reform took over in 1913, prisoners weren't allowed outdoors. There was no prison yard. Think about it—one hour for outside recreation per year (on the fourth of July). Closed by the state in 2002, the prison is known as a backdrop to the 1980 movie, *Blues Brothers*. After falling prey to vandals, the city of Joliet took over management of this pre–Civil War prison campus, and now tours are offered by Joliet Area Historical Museum. Roofs have fallen in and graffiti covers surfaces, but the history is there. Some tour guides are former Joliet Prison guards.

A new beginning for this prison is the inaugural Blues Brothers Con, held in 2022, an event that featured a performance by Dan Akroyd (Elwood Blues) and Jim Belushi (brother to John, aka, Joliet Jake). The Joliet Historical Museum intends to continue this event into the future, with proceeds buttressing efforts to maintain prison grounds.

1125 Collins St., Joliet, 312-978-1282
jolietprison.org

VIEW
A VIKING SHIP

When an intact, ancient Viking ship was found buried on a farm in Norway in 1880, Scandinavians went wild because it proved Viking expertise and buttressed conjectures about Norse explorer Leif Erikson having led the first Europeans to North America. Wanting to shout the news to the world, the unearthed ship served as a template for a replica built for the 1893 Chicago World's Fair. Sailing from Norway to Chicago, it went on display for all to see. Afterward, the ship was housed at the Field Museum and later in Lincoln Park. Today, it resides in a shelter built by "Friends of the Viking Ship" in Geneva. The "Friends" hope to build a permanent museum in Geneva by 2025. Tours take place seasonally, beginning with a talk, then guests file inside the shelter and climb a platform, allowing a view inside the boat. This is when it hits you—what amount of muscle pulled those oars from Norway to North America?

Ship's shelter is at Good Templar Park
528 East Side Dr., Geneva
vikingship.us

TIP

Good Templar Park is also home to a collection of stugas (Swedish cottages), privately owned, but open to the public on Midsommar—a Swedish holiday that marks the longest day of the year. For unique lodging in Geneva, Oscar Swan House is a mansion with lots of options.

WELCOME HOME VETERANS
FROM AN HONOR FLIGHT (STATEWIDE)

Conveying gratitude to veterans who have served in past wars is gratifying, and one of the most meaningful ways to do so is by welcoming them home from an Honor Flight. Founded in 2005, the Honor Flight Network brings veterans to Washington, DC, to visit memorials and monuments built in their honor. After their whirlwind day, Illinois veterans land at one of five airports—including Midway-Chicago, Peoria International, Williamson County Regional-Marion, Capital Airport-Springfield, and Quad Cities International-Moline.

Many veterans, especially those from the Vietnam era, did not receive a warm welcome after fighting overseas. This is your chance to light up a veteran's face. Honor Flight Chicago held their 100th flight in April 2022, and other Honor Flight chapters around the state offer five or six flights per year. Put one of these Welcome Home moments on your calendar for an unforgettable experience.

Honor Flight Chicago
773-227-8387
honorflightchicago.org

Greater Peoria Honor Flight
309-397-6975
greaterpeoriahonorflight.org

Honor Flight Quad Cities
563-388-3592
honorflightqc.org

Land of Lincoln Honor Flight (Springfield)
217-585-1219 or 217-652-4719
landoflincolnhonorflight.org

Veterans Honor Flight
(Williamson County/Marion)
618-942-3930
veteranshonorflight.org

VISIT
BLACK HAWK STATE HISTORIC SITE

The Sauk warrior Black Hawk lived where Rock Island is now. He and his people (Sauks and Fox) lived in Saukenuk, which was the largest village in Illinois through the 1820s. As Anglo-Americans moved closer to the village, clashes occurred and the federal government stepped in. The Indian Removal Act of 1830 enforced the removal of all tribes to areas west of the Mississippi, including the residents of Saukenuk. Black Hawk insisted that a treaty signed decades earlier was not binding since it was signed by four lower chiefs, who didn't have authority to cede ancestral lands. Black Hawk said, "I wish to remain where the bones of my fathers are laid." But that was not to be. Black Hawk Historic Site includes the Hauberg Indian Museum, housed in a lodge built by the Civilian Conservation Corps (1934), a park, and trails. The Hauberg Museum interprets the culture of the once mighty Sauk with replicas of winter and summer houses and life-size figures engaged in activities common to their culture. The history of the tribes who dwelled across Illinois could fill sets of encyclopedias, and this museum offers lessons about an important era.

1510 46th Ave., Rock Island, 309-788-0177
blackhawkpark.org

TIP

The Rock River stretches from the IL/ Wisconsin state line near Rockford to the IL/ Iowa state line near Rock Island; about midway along the river valley is Lowden State Park in Oregon, with a 48-foot statue of Black Hawk atop a bluff—viewable from the Oregon side (Rt. 2) or up close within the state park.

TAKE A TRIP
THROUGH THE FRENCH CANADIAN CORRIDOR

If your roots are French Canadian, you're likely linked (as is Angelina Jolie) to the corridor that stretches along I-57 in Kankakee and Iroquois Counties. Signs at the exits for Manteno and Ashkum delineate this area where early French fur traders lived alongside the Potawatomi. At the north end of the corridor, the village of Bourbonnais is named for French Canadian Francois Bourbonnais Sr. Here, village welcome signs bear the French symbol, fleur-de-lis. The French Heritage Museum, located in Kankakee's historic Stone Barn, is operated under the auspices of the Kankakee County Museum and tells of pioneers whose roots track to Canada, France, and Belgium. From the museums to churches that catered to the French in this area (including the National Shrine of St. Anne) to the unincorporated community of L'Erable (French for maple), this area is a destination for anyone wanting to understand the strong French influence across Illinois.

Bourbonnais Museum
bourbonnaishistory.org/french-canadian-corridor

French Heritage Museum
165 N Indiana Ave., Kankakee (open April through December)

Kankakee County Museum
801 S 8th Ave., Kankakee, 815-932-5279

TIP

In L'Erable is the iconic Longbranch Restaurant, and just to its south is an ex-hideout of Al Capone's. Going south from the Longbranch to the stop sign at Rt. 52, you'll see twin farmhouses that were the guardhouses. Capone's old hideout is beyond those houses, along the Iroquois River (look for the slitted upper windows).

Christkindlmarket in Daley Plaza, Chicago

SHOPPING AND FASHION

SHOP IN THE HEART
OF AMISH COUNTRY

As Illinois's oldest Amish settlement, Arthur's Vine Street shops offer the stuff of dreams. Want made-to-order furniture? It's here, with workmanship that withstands the test of time. From the Visitor Center (corner of Vine and Progress Streets), the shops extend south along Vine, with furniture shops selling quilts, flower shops offering yummy fudge, and a home goods store with chic skirts and purses. Yoder's Lamps & Antiques has a bit of everything from hand-fashioned textile crafts to antique weather vanes. Arthur General Store is actually two trendy shops under one ownership where you'll find chemical-free lotions made on-site (ask to meet the guy behind the curtain . . . he's often in the back!). Expect to spend two to three hours on Vine Street. Then, with a map from the Visitor Center, explore more shops on other streets, some in town, some in the country. To keep up your energy, try Yoder's Kitchen, where you'll find pot roast that melts in your mouth as well as country fresh pies. Oh my!

TIP

If you decide to stay overnight in the area, check Airbnb for local flavor. Also, be sure to zip six miles east of Arthur to Arcola, home to Yoder's Homestead, a huge store with gifts, crafts, and locally made jams.

FIND ALL YOUR NOTIONS
AT THREADS OF TIME
SEWING AND RETREAT CENTER

Quilters take their craft seriously, and so does the Threads of Time Sewing Center. Here, you'll find thousands of bolts of fabric, notions, sewing machines, craft kits, and precuts in all shapes, sizes, and colors. They stock designers and brands that are all the rage—all at your fingertips. Plus, they offer craft classes for those with varying skills sets. And should you so choose, you can literally stitch from dawn till dusk by booking a stay at their 36-bed retreat center. Their large sewing room offers tons of table space, so that you might just make a new friend or two while you sew. For years, satisfied customers have traveled great distances to get here. How far will you drive?

207 S Buchanan St., Danville, 217-431-9202
threadsoftimefab.com

TIP

Another unique way to stay in the Danville area is the Has Bin in Alvin, where you can sleep in a grain bin converted into a cozy BnB. With a second story loft that steps out onto a deck overlooking (what else?) cornfields, you'll feel a million miles from Monday.

thehasbinguesthouse.com

SHOP THE MAGNIFICENT MILE IN CHICAGO

Thirteen blocks of pure magnificence welcome tourists from around the world to Chicago. Dubbed the "Mag Mile," this mecca of commerce runs along Michigan Avenue from the Chicago River to Oak Street. There are fashion hotspots such as Nordstrom and Neiman Marcus, the Signature Room Restaurant on the 95th floor of the historic John Hancock Building, and the Broadway Playhouse at Water Tower Place. For an extra high, hit the TILT on the Hancock's 94th floor observation deck, one of planet Earth's highest thrill rides. A newbie (sort of) to the Mag Mile is Starbucks Roastery, where "immersion experience" is the buzz phrase. Four floors cater to patrons' mood of the day (or night). Also along the Mag Mile is one of the few structures that survived the Chicago Fire of 1871, the gothic Water Tower and Pumping Station. If it's open, step inside.

The annual Mag Mile Festival of Lights parade kicks off the holiday season with the largest nighttime parade in the nation. Led by Mickey and Minnie, the parade's one million lights illuminate the Mag Mile's 200 trees. What a great way to celebrate.

themagnificentmile.com

FIND MILES OF SHOPS
AT GURNEE MILLS

With nearly 200 stores, a movie theater, restaurants (including the ever popular Rainforest Café), and an indoor ice skating rink, Gurnee Mills is one of the largest malls in America. Anchored by big name stores such as Macy's and Bass Pro Shops, and with several outlet stores including Adidas and Abercrombie Kids, if you cannot find it here, you may consider the possibility that it does not exist. Since this mall is all on one level, in order to breeze by all the stores, park near Macy's or Burlington so that you can make a sweep from one end to the other. Without counting backtracks, the entire Z-shaped path through the mall is 2.3 kilometers or 1.43 miles. Choose your most comfortable walking shoes.

6170 W Grand Ave., Gurnee
simon.com/gurnee-mills

TIP

For outlet malls, hit Fashion Outlets in Rosemont or Chicago Premium Outlets in Aurora. They are absolutely the bomb.

SOAK UP GERMAN CULTURE AT CHRISTKINDLMARKET

People from across the Midwest trek to this mecca of German culture and commerce, which has been held at Daley Plaza in downtown Chicago since 1996. Christkindlmarket is an open-air German marketplace offering the greatest array of German culture in one place in Illinois, and has been dubbed the most authentic holiday market of its kind outside of Europe. There are handcrafted glass-blown ornaments, toys carved of wood, and various items made of porcelain, lace, paper, and more. From nutcrackers and cuckoo clocks (mini to large) to thermal pyramids and carved beer steins, they're here. And of course, no German marketplace is complete without Lebkuchen (large heart shaped gingerbread cookies given more often as gifts than eaten). Vendors sell potato pancakes, bratwurst, and glühwein (hot mulled spiced wine), and there's entertainment that continues throughout this 30-day festival. Running from the weekend before Thanksgiving right up to Christmas Eve (day), Christkindlmarket is like going to Germany, but without the transatlantic flight.

Daley Plaza
50 W Washington, Chicago, 312-494-2175
christkindlmarket.com

TIP

If you drive, opt to reserve a spot ahead of time at Grant Park-North garage, where parking on a Friday evening, "up to eight hours," costs about $17; the garage is just a few blocks from Daley Plaza.

millenniumgarages.com

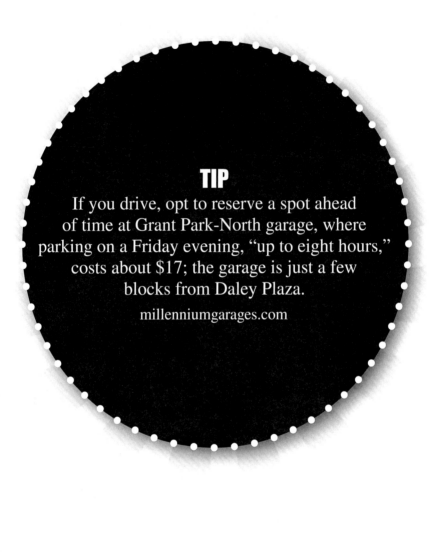

FIND A GIFT TO UPLIFT THE HUMAN SPIRIT

AT LAMB'S FARM

A visit to Lamb's Farm is a must for many reasons. What began in 1961 as a pet shop in Chicago, with the owners staffing the store with adults with developmental disabilities, is now a facility on what was once a 70-acre family farm. A farm donated for this mecca of the human spirit. In addition to a residential section, Lamb's Farm has a farmyard, restaurant, and three shops, all of which support their residents in leading productive lives by offering options to work in front-office places or behind the scenes.

At their Sugar Maple Country Store, you'll find candies, jams, teas, lotions, and bath bombs. Magnolia Café & Bakery is open daily for dining. Their Cedar Chest Thrift Shop contains some of the best treasures, with donations from caring (and affluent) folks who have long supported the Lamb's Farm mission at prices you must see to believe. And their crowning jewel, Dogwood Garden & Pet Center, offers pet adoptions year-round. When you shop here, you are supporting a community of care—and there's no better gift than that.

14245 W Rockland Rd., Libertyville, 847-362-4636
lambsfarm.org

TIP

When you pull into Lamb's Farm, use the big parking lot on the right. The farmyard is there, and when you cross the road, you'll find the café and pathways to the shops. Public restrooms are next to the pavilion.

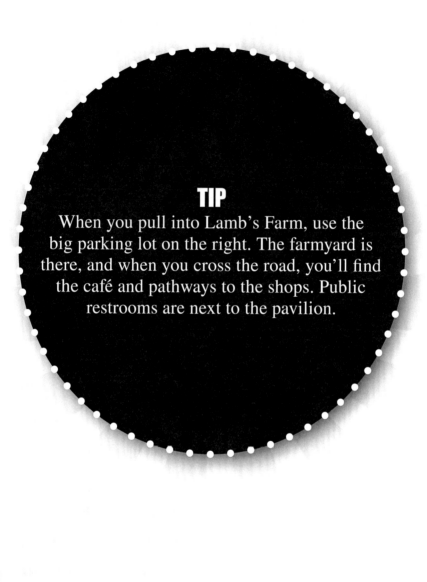

95

EXPLORE NORTHERN ILLINOIS'S LARGEST ANTIQUE MALL

You could get lost for days inside the Grand Antique Company's 28,000 square feet of space. Housed in a historic beauty of a building that was built as a community school in 1900, these walls hold many memories. Not just in what they sell, but in the stories of the schoolchildren who learned their 3 R's there for more than a century. With 200 vendor booths brimming with vintage items, there are collectibles, handicrafts, plus walls (and walls) of books, and more. There's so much here that the folks at *Midwest Living* (2022) and *House Beautiful* (2021) got it right when they called this place "special." Fifteen miles from Galena, and just steps from scenic Route 20, Elizabeth's Grand Antique Co. is a destination not to be missed.

300 West St., Elizabeth, 815-858-9477
grandantiqueco.com

OTHER ANTIQUE MALLS THAT SHOULD BE ON YOUR RADAR

Olde Timers Antique Centre
Three floors and 25,000 sq. ft. of pure antique bliss
113 E Church St., Sandwich, 815-786-6430

Wabash Depot Antique Center
Inside a restored, landmark-status rail depot, with 10,000 sq. ft. of treasures
780 E Cerro Gordo, Decatur, 217-233-0800

El Paso Antique Mall
Just off I-39, a warehouse-style antique mall
15 Linco Dr., El Paso, 309-527-3705

Bushert's Antiques
Bushert's has the largest collection of antique furniture in central Illinois
13 Westgate Dr., El Paso

Ten Pin Antique Mall
Located in an old bowling alley, you can now walk on the old lanes. "One million pieces" for sale in this 11,000 sq. ft. space . . . if the walls could talk
11515 State Rt. 127, Carlyle, 618-792-9709

Countree Peddler
Deemed the largest antique store in the southernmost tip of Illinois
605 W Main St., Goreville, 618-995-9222

Manteno Antique Mall
With over 100 dealers, great finds, great prices.
35 E 3rd St., Manteno, 815-468-0114

SEE THE "SEA OF CHINA"

AT HOFFMAN'S PATTERNS OF THE PAST

In 1944, Allen Murphey began a business finding replacement pieces for discontinued tableware. Almost seven decades later, the store is still family-owned, and it holds 275,000 patterns of china and 15,000 crystal types—95 percent of which are brand new items. So sought after are their designs that they regularly ship pieces around the world. Owned and operated by Murphey's children, they lovingly call the store their father started the "Sea of China." (So many patterns!) And they say, "We'll be here another 100 years!" This store is much more than a china shop. There are collectibles, holiday items, cookie jars, clocks, Swarovski, the list goes on. Walking amid Hoffman's "sea" is a bit like a time machine, transporting you to the store shelves of 50 years ago.

513 S Main St., Princeton, 815-875-1944
patternsofthepast.com

TIP

While you're in Princeton, see the state's oldest covered bridge, built in 1863, on County Rd. 1950E, just off Rt. 26. Follow Main/Rt. 26 north from I-80, then turn west on Rt. 1950E.

BUY WESTERN WEAR FROM THE BEST

AT BOTH ENDS OF THE STATE

When shopping for cowboy boots, hats, or other western wear, go to the best. In northern Illinois, that would be Alcala's Western Wear in Chicago, and in southern Illinois, it's McKinney's Western Store in Marion. Both are family-owned shops with decades-long reputations. Each store draws western wear lovers from near and far and offers cute boots for kids, Stetsons or Twisters (hats) for adults, vests, chaps, belts, and lots more.

Whereas McKinney's in Marion serves a clientele that needs feed supplies, Alcala's is an urban oasis of the Wild West where you might find a python skin money belt or elegant Charro dress.

McKinney's Western Store is a stone's throw from I-57, not far from Southern Illinois University. Alcala's is in Chicago's West Town neighborhood, about four blocks west of I-90/I-94 Expressway. Note that Alcala's has their own parking lot, across the street—look for a sign with a bucking horse with a rider on its back (the store has its own bucking horse on its storefront, go farther west to the next horse).

Alcala's
1733 W Chicago Ave., Chicago
312-226-0152
alcalas.com

McKinney's
802 Halfway Rd., Marion
618-997-6974
mckinneyswesternstore.com

DISCOVER THE QUAINT SHOPS OF HISTORIC LONG GROVE

Once a German farming settlement, Long Grove long ago saw the expansion of Main Street USA, with its razing of history and erection of connected storefronts, as something to be avoided. So, they passed ordinances about what could be built. The result is a collection of quaint shops, some housed in historic barns. There are confectioneries, candy stores, gift shops, artisan repositories, wineries, and more. If you haven't been to Long Grove lately, you might not know that sidewalks were added in 2019, making these shops much easier to navigate. A trip here is even better during one of Long Grove's festivals, such as the Chocolate Fest (May) or Apple Fest (September).

A one-of-a-kind place is the Sock Monkey Museum, designed by Arlene Okun, whose affinity for the "lovey" that rose in popularity during the Great Depression, inspired this place. With a museum on the second floor (fun for all ages), there's a humongous collection of sock monkeys, one of which stopped a customer in her tracks—who lingered over a sock monkey that looked like the one her grandma gave her decades earlier. (Be aware that there are stairs to the second level.)

Shops radiate out from the intersection of Old McHenry Rd. and Robert Parker Coffin Rd., two blocks from Long Grove's historic covered bridge
longgrove.org

ATTEND
PRINTERS ROW LIT FEST IN CHICAGO

When it comes to books, nothing in the Midwest compares to Chicago's annual Printers Row Lit Fest. This huge, free, outdoor literary event is where publishers, big and small, set up tents filled with books and some of the authors who wrote them. Located in Printers Row (a three block by three block area), this was once the mecca of the printing and bookbinding world, churning out hundreds of thousands of magazines, catalogs, and the like. So, when the book world looks for a place in which to set up an open air festival, they come here. This two-day affair offers over 100 authors who participate in panels and programs (indoors at Jones College Prep High School). And after each program ends, book lovers can get in line to meet the author. If you love books (please say you do!) and want a chance to say hello to some of the folks who put print to the pages you read, Printers Row Lit Fest is the place to be.

Bounded by Ida B. Wells Drive to the north, State Street to the east, Polk Street to the south, Clark to the west.
printersrowlitfest.org

TIP

If you take the Metra-Rock Island line to LaSalle Str. Station, take the east (right-hand) exit out of the station, turn right at the bottom of the escalators, then left onto Ida B. Wells Drive, and walk one block east to the festival. Voila!

SHOP
AT WOMEN & CHILDREN FIRST

Opened in 1979, and now one of America's largest feminist bookstores, Women & Children First (W&CF) hung up its shingle when the second Women's Movement was just simmering down. Located in the heart of Chicago's Andersonville neighborhood, W&CF's mission is as crucial as it was over 40 years earlier—to feature women writers and foster discussions of feminist issues and culture. And of course, they nurture children's love of literature through story times, programs, and well-stocked shelves. Though hosting women authors aligns with their core values, their true impact is felt in their store, which touts 20,000 books by and about women, books for children, and the best in LGBTQ lit. Here is where you're sure to find a book that uplifts, informs, matters.

5233 N Clark St., Chicago, 773-769-9299
womenandchildrenfirst.com

TIP

There are independent brick-and-mortar bookstores that deserve our patronage. This means calling your local bookstore and asking them to order that book you're looking for. (Please do it. We need them.)

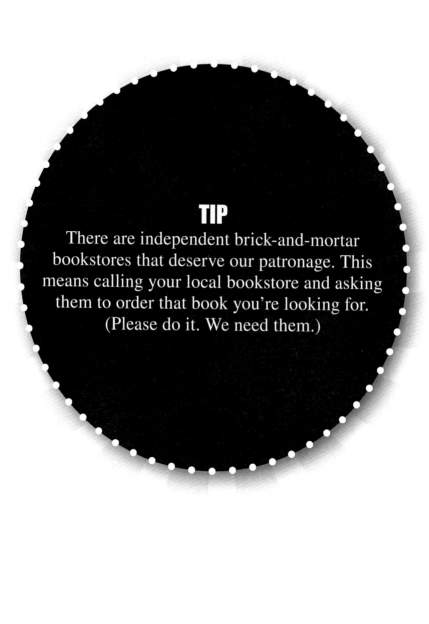

Cave-In-Rock

SUGGESTED ITINERARIES

FOR THRILL SEEKERS

PERFECT FOR KIDS

CALLING MUSIC LOVERS

CULTURAL EXPERIENCES

SPORTS FANS

FRESH AIR SPOTS

WONDERFULLY OFF-THE-WALL

ANIMAL AFICIONADOS

HISTORY BUFFS

ON THE WATER

THE HOUSE OF THE LORD
THE CHURCH OF JESUS CHRIST
OF LATTER-DAY SAINTS
HOLINESS TO THE LORD
Nauvoo Illinois Temple

Pioneer Village, Quinsippi Island, Quincy

ACTIVITIES
BY SEASON

WINTER

SPRING

SUMMER

FALL

Starved Rock State Park, Wildcat Canyon
Photo by Joe Jakupcak

INDEX